ON THE RUN

ON THE RUN

Finding the Trail Home

CATHERINE DOUCETTE

Oregon State University Press   Corvallis

Library of Congress Cataloging-in-Publication Data

Names: Doucette, Catherine, author.
Title: On the run : finding the trail home / Catherine Doucette.
Description: Corvallis : Oregon State University Press, 2021.
Identifiers: LCCN 2020057099 | ISBN 9780870713002 (trade paperback)
   | ISBN 9780870713019 (ebook)
Subjects: LCSH: Doucette, Catherine. | Outdoor life—United States.
   | Women—United States—Social conditions. | Outdoorswomen—
   United States—Biography.
Classification: LCC GV191.52.D68 A3 2021 | DDC 796.50973—dc23
LC record available at https://lccn.loc.gov/2020057099

♾ This paper meets the requirements of ANSI/NISO Z39.48-1992
(Permanence of Paper).

 **Oregon State University**
OSU Press

Oregon State University Press
121 The Valley Library
Corvallis OR 97331-4501
541-737-3166 • fax 541-737-3170
www.osupress.oregonstate.edu

For my family

CONTENTS

ACKNOWLEDGMENTS

This book never would have been possible without the support and kindness of many people in my life. I am indebted to innumerable family members, friends, editors, and instructors—too many to chronicle here. I do want to say thank you in particular to my dear friend, Dio, who read every word more than once; to Jessie, who provided invaluable, years-long support; to Bob, Tracy, Ted, and Marjorie for their thoughtful guidance from the beginning. I am very fortunate to be surrounded by a network of such loving, smart, and strong people.

Previously published essays:
"Church of the Atavists" in *The Ski Journal*, Volume 5.1, Fall 2011 (print)
"When the Lake Makes Ice" in *Silk Road Review*, Spring 2012 (print)
"The Weight of Healing" in *Bellingham Review*, Issue 65, Fall 2012 (online)
"Roots" in *Emrys Journal*, Spring 2013 (print)
"On the Run" in *The Emerson Review*, Spring 2013 (print/online)
"Herd Animals" in *The Los Angeles Review*, Fall 2013 (print)
"Into the Bite" in *The South Dakota Review*, Spring 2015 (print)

WHEN THE LAKE MAKES ICE

I can no longer remember the first time I heard the ice booming on a frigid night. That exact moment eludes me, not so much slipped from my mind as fused into the layers of childhood memory, bound to the accumulations of the past.

I grew up on the steely edges of Forest Lake in the White Mountains of New Hampshire. There was something silent and selfish about winters for me. Our home, and my grandmother's home just two doors down, were the only winter residences on our side of the lake. Although the bulging dirt road was plowed for us in the wintertime, the rumble of the plow rarely broke our winter slumber. We were not the town's main concern. The summer folk had stowed their canoes upside down, drained their water pipes, locked and shuttered their windows, and pulled their docks up on the sandy shoreline. In the winter months of my childhood, the lake belonged to me again. Only the occasional cross-country skier, ice fisherman, or snowmobiler trespassed on my white oval. Otherwise, and especially at night, the lake was mine.

During snapping cold nights, my dad zipped up his old gray coat, laced his battered hockey skates, and ducked out the front door. Alongside our dock was the outline of a rectangle of ice, snow banks heaping around the edges. Grabbing the rusted scoop shovel, he would methodically scrape the rink free of snow. Although I couldn't always see the push and glide of my father's figure, a six-foot frame hunched against the shovel and the night, I could hear the scrape of the metal blade against the cold surface. The rink looked like a carefully tended field, rows of shovel marks disappearing into the nighttime. Once it was cleared, he dipped five-gallon buckets through a hand-chopped hole. Skating out with the buckets dripping, he threw the dark water onto the ice. Cool lake water flooded the cracks and seeped into the gaps. The spotlight, attached to the house, cast Dad in thin shadows as he worked to create this space for us. Only on the coldest nights would he be out flooding, which would even out the ice, eliminate the friction, and restore the rink. We awoke to smooth surfaces refreshed by work and water.

∧ ∧ ∧

But this is how a skating rink is maintained, not how the lake builds that thick plate of ice each year. The lake forms skims of ice that first cling to the dock and shore close to home, and eventually reach out to cover the whole expanse of water. Frosty fingers stretch away from the shore to creep into the deeper waters, growing and spreading until they join with ice from the opposite shore, far in the distance, to form the first delicate skin. That is how it begins.

New ice accumulates one layer at a time. But it is created from below. Water is the only known nonmetallic substance that expands when it freezes, and younger layers of fresh ice push the existing ice upward, splitting it like an old skin that no longer fits but refuses to be shed. The oldest ice is on top, history turned upside down to expose the cracks of the past. Fractures shoot and explode across the plate, reverberating like snapping cables. It is an oddly electronic and far-reaching report in the night air.

∧ ∧ ∧

The first thin sheet would send us to the closet to dig out skates, fingering the sharpness of the blades. In the evenings after dinner, when darkness coated the landscape, my dad would lace up my hockey skates. Kneeling in front of the woodstove, he pulled and tied the long cotton laces. Then I would wobble on the blades over the carpet and slice across the porch, down the beach, and finally glide out onto the rink. Skating on cracking cold evenings, we could hear the lake making new ice, heaving the surface upwards. Our shadows, cast from the porch light, would melt into the darkness as we skated steadily away from home.

∧ ∧ ∧

Just when the ice began clinging to the shores, we took our seasonal trip to Littleton, New Hampshire, the next town over, to go see Mr. Stefekos. He was a compact man with a basement full of used hockey skates. As we grew from year to year, we traded in our old pairs for new ones. The empty skates lined the room, several rows deep with the smell of leather and heat. After we put on thick winter socks and jammed our eager feet into several pairs, Dad would settle on a cluster of skates to take home. Then we would watch Mr. Stefekos sharpen them. Sparks shot from the machine as the buzz spoke of the honing. The blade, shiny and sharp, would be ready to score the even surface of our rink. For years we had a hard time remembering what skates belonged to what child; both were constantly changing. Eventually our feet stopped growing and found permanent homes in the thin black leather of hockey skates, the laces fat with use. Even now our skates wait in the dented boot box for our wintertime visits to the icy playground of our youth. There is some reassurance in returning to that thick place of past, to the secure yet impermanent surfaces of wintertime.

^ ^ ^

Ice is less dense than water, and the first skims of ice float to the surface, gathering into a sheet that protects a whole ecosystem hidden below. Despite the often-violent expansion of ice creation, the sheet ultimately insulates and preserves. Cracks ooze with water and seal again, scarred, but better able to bear weight. Raised ribbons weld the lake together until the next snap of growth. The building layers that fracture with each cold heave make the lake more stable and protect the life still thrumming below the surface.

^ ^ ^

As children, we would lay our muffled ears against the hard ice and wait for the boom. Sharp stars kept us company. Then a sonic thump would buckle the lake from below. Thick shots of sound exploded and ricocheted through the ice. Our whole bodies rocked with the transformation. We could feel the ice growing beneath us. We knew that despite the cracks, it was building. As a child I found it hard to believe. How could something be getting stronger by splitting apart?

^ ^ ^

My dad long ago stopped maintaining an ice rink. He has aged, and the bitter nights no longer beg his attention, nor do insistent children, who have scattered. But when I returned home for the holidays in 2005, the lake had done the job for him. In a rare thaw-freeze cycle, the ice froze smooth and no snow blanketed the skating surface. Still jet-lagged after my flight from Switzerland, where I was halfway through my first year of teaching, I tightened my own skates to head out. Coming home for Christmas and finding the lake perfect for skating felt like being caught and coddled, a sweet return to childhood and the familiar, so far away from the foreign teaching adventures that had spun my recent life.

Dad, Mom, and I cruised effortlessly over the mirrored oval together. I stooped to look through the ice, my jeans growing cold at the knees, and peered into a black sheet. The ice was clear enough to see into, thick enough to carry our weight, and strong enough even for remembering. It held smooth and supportive against my skate blades.

As I stood still and balanced, I watched my parents, off a little way, holding hands, their big mittens bulky in their union. I followed them with my eyes, their heads tilted together, their strokes steady. With a shift in my weight, my blades scored the ice in a circle and I turned to look homeward. Nestled between soaring pines was the house, right on the shore where the ice is strongest. From this distance it was easier to take in the scene. Although I have lived away from here in recent years, my sense of belonging to this place has built like the slips of ice that harden into a thick sheet. I trust that this process will hold. I have come to understand it better, having lived the logic in the strength of fracture. That night, I felt the house buck when the ice boomed, a sound I have never heard anywhere but home.

IN THE CHURCH OF THE ATAVISTS

Traveling by foot in the mountains seems ancestral, back to the days of our predecessors where the earth splayed open, inviting exploration. A time when people had to rely on their bodies, each other, and the accumulated knowledge of their past. This has changed for the most part. Dark roads penetrate the vast wilderness, cars chug up hills, fuel stations appear in even the most remote folds of our world. But there are still places where you can look out into the mountains and see only the imprint of nature. The Chugatch Range in Alaska is one of these places.

I find myself there, just outside of Valdez, blissfully close to the wilderness for a three-week backcountry ski trip. In response to a picture that I send my Dad of this mountainous place, he writes, "Looks like beautiful country. You are in the church of the atavists."

^ ^ ^

Once assembled, we are four men, one woman, two sets of siblings. Hulking duffels, seven pairs of skis, enough gear for three weeks in the backcountry, and five eager bodies are crammed into the minivan. Cigarette burns dot the upholstery and the glovebox sways in the dash. I feel exactly where I belong, drawn here for a reason. I drive through Thompson Pass in the dark. Everyone else fades in and out of sleep. I can feel the dark beings of the mountains closing in around me, hear the grind of the engine and the wet rhythm of the studded tires on the minivan. The massive shards of earth, referred to collectively as the Chugach, stand in relief against the moon, the snow leaping out in the light.

∧ ∧ ∧

We are backcountry skiers; we move ourselves through the wilderness. We have skied hard enough over the last five days to flatten our energy, our muscles, and our remaining ambition. My legs ache. I don't look in the mirror often these days, but I know what I look like. My cheekbones are tinged pink-brown with wind and sun. My blond hair is dented in the pattern of a braid—the best way to keep my hair back and comfortable under a helmet. I know my frame looks tall, nearly six feet, and perhaps skinnier than I actually am with a hip belt cinched close over my waist. Even on off days I dress in layers—wool and fleece—and I blend with the rest of my companions in every aspect except gender. We all have slight sunburns and it looks like we have survived something. So, we take a rest day to tinker with gear, catch up on email, and eat our weight in food. The group composition—I am the lone woman—surprises some people, although it is not all that unusual for backcountry crews. Both my brothers, Peter and Jim, are along. With us are the Rossi brothers, Silas and Saben. Silas and my older brother, Peter, are friends and guides. The group is a family. We move as one herd and are rarely spaced far enough apart to lose eye contact.

As we sink into eating and resting, I read the email from my dad and am forced to ask if anyone knows the definition of atavist. We are five college graduates, three English majors among us, and yet no one has a clue what atavism is. I plug it in online to see what "church" my dad thinks we are in, exactly. The word has to do with science mostly, that an ancestral trait has resurfaced after generations of being absent—like a tail showing up on a baby. But really, I realize that my dad is right, we are praying in the church of our ancestors, because when we look out over that snow-laden mountain scene, we are seeing it through the eyes of the people who first saw it. We are moving back to a time when the world was younger.

Mountains move slowly, so as I turn my face to look at the stacked peaks, I see what people centuries ago must have seen—glaciers that edge the ridges with long streaks of snow running from each pinnacle, summit, and flank. The bodies of these mountains have nothing on them but our eyes and the blanket of weather and time. And as I look around, I see my brothers and the Rossis consuming the same vistas. I inherently trust them in this moment. We are original to this experience; I feel it resonate in my own history.

This club is exclusive. Backcountry skiers are rare, especially around Valdez, Alaska. The rotors of helicopters continually beat the winter air as we ski. Snowmobiles whine in the distance; somewhere over the next ridge a snowcat grinds at the snow. It takes an interesting mix of traits to motivate a person to want to move her own body into the mountains, to take responsibility for travel, to attain without assistance. We are a tight little group; we rely on each other.

The list of qualifications is vast. For me to feel comfortable in the backcountry, partners must be strong. Companions have restless legs in the face of powder. Their stamina is significant, and they have the ability to climb for a long day. They own and know how to use a beacon, probe, and shovel. They must be acquainted with snow intimately and have a healthy fear of avalanches. They frequently ask questions about the terrain, the snow pack, the route, how people are feeling, and if we should stop to eat. A love for mountains, sweat, and travel is required. A hunger for snow and gravity and slope is innate in their character. Humor helps to tie together the best experiences. Partners take responsibility for themselves—from managing exposure on a ridgeline, to wearing sunglasses and sunscreen, hydrating, and knowing their limits. They boast knowledge and experience and are bootpack champions. I trust them with my mistakes or theirs, because we are watching out for one another. Each member adds something special, like Peter and Silas, who help us navigate the big mountains of our dreams, making choices based on safety and thrill.

Partners are versed in the language of the mountains. Words like sluff and skins, couloir and randonee roll easily in their minds. Sublimation, depth hoar, propagation, and sheer test are the language of our interactions, because we need to be able to communicate. The best companions are elusive, spending their time at the outer edges of the world. And here we have assembled to pray to the snow and mountain gods.

In order to find comfort among the big bodies of the mountains, bloated with fresh snow, I need to be able to trust my team with my own weakness. Exposure of vulnerability is the thing that I fear most among my backcountry brethren, but it is only when I can trust them with my honest reflexes that we bond. Like snow on a slope, the bonds of stability are crucial. It's easy to tell you about the highlights of a ski trip, the massive storms, the turns, the sunshine, and the company. But I can pinpoint the moment when I was sure I belonged.

It was supposed to be a rest day on what otherwise would have been our fifth ski day in a row. But because the weather forecast called for sun, with the days following predicted to be rainy with poor visibility, the good weather forced us out the door. I understood the call—squeeze one more day in before weather bound us to the valley. But every ache in my body resisted getting up early and skiing back toward the glacier, Peak 5802, and the damned persistent wind and sun.

We gathered at Thompson Pass and layered against the elements. Our two-hour skin into the couloir happened mostly in silence. My legs were heavy, and my mind, despite the radiant sunshine, resisted the ascent. I was okay all the way up to the base of the couloir, where the ramp flattens into clean snow, dotted with roller-ball trails and debris from the left wall. I was cold—I should say that, too. My wet, leather gloves clung to my dying hands as I flicked and shook them to get my circulation back. I kept going and pounded a Snickers bar and Gatorade with hope.

Halfway up the tongue of the mountain, in the shadow of the ridge, I hit a wall. For the first time in the trip I wanted to cry and wondered if I might. Crying has never been my inclination, having grown up in a stoic New England culture, so I fought that impulse in the below-zero temperatures of the mountain flank. My hands stung and failed to flex in what I imagined was a normal way. They loosely clutched my poles, caught in mid-stride up the bootpack. Each step came more slowly as I realized that I was unhappy. Really unhappy. I stopped and kicked my feet into the steep ramp. Looking up the shady couloir, I yelled to Jim, "Can you tell Pete and Silas I am done?" I didn't want to move. I did want my down jacket, my mittens, and more to eat. The group stopped and I managed the twenty-two steps up to them.

Silas dug a deep shelf into the body of the slabby couloir. We all set about transitioning, halfway up the slip of snow, in the shade of the day. They said they wanted to turn around because of the snow— both the stability and the quality. The whole slope was a study in slab. And it was, but I don't know what percentage of the decision was an excuse to make me feel better. I had halted the ascent. Of course, I offered to bundle up and wait while they finished climbing. My impulse to cry had receded. Knowing when and how to turn around deserves consideration and can be the most important part of the day. For me, this turning point was essential. My group refused to leave me, and one by one we skied the shot to the bottom and into the glorious sunlight again.

We bid our farewell to Peak 5802 and did not lap. This smaller day was because of me and my fear that I was dangerously tired and I could get hurt. But the creeping threat had faded with the emergence of the sun and the return of my humor. We skied light, delightful snow to the road. I ditched my "scowl," as Peter called it, and we left the mountains for the day. As a group, they did not leave me tucked into the side of the mountain to wait. The boys took my exposed vulnerability as part of their own experience and turned in the shade with me. This is how I knew I belonged, because I could speak in my own voice, even when claiming weakness.

I have always been drawn to the mountains and the brand of people I find in them. There is a quality of person who appreciates the quiet of a landscape. I believe that in the map of my history there were people who first opened their eyes to the mountains and felt nourished. Perhaps we are not related. Theirs is not a branch on my ancestral tree, but somehow I have found their progeny. Jim, Peter, Silas, Saben, and I are all innately connected, not because we went on this trip together, but because we find solace in the outdoors. Each of us has taken steps to qualify ourselves as parishioners in the church of the atavists.

ONE OF THE BOYS

We cram twelve skiers into three rooms at The Alpine Motel in Nelson, British Columbia. It's early 2013 and we have chosen this motel because it is the cheapest option around, and they won't ask how many people we will put in each room. Once we are moved in for the night, we pile into one room and pass around the cheapest bottle of vodka you can get in Canada. In a plastic jug, the clear liquor tastes the way I imagine turpentine must taste, burning. Aaron has the giggles. With the bottle in his hand, he turns to me and says, "I can't believe you came on this trip. Aren't you uncomfortable?" Chris grabs the bottle from him and says, "Dude, saying that will make her uncomfortable!" The others echo this sentiment. "Yeah, come on, Aaron!"

Once again, on the cusp of a ski trip, I find myself happily settled into a group of good men. The numbers are impressive this year. Even more disproportionate than usual. I am the only woman in the group of twelve. I am about to be dropped into the backcountry for a week of earn-your-turns skiing with eleven men. And I can't wait. I've been skiing and laughing with variations of this group for years. My skiing and social abilities have been established. I stand up for myself, and I'm not easily offended. I can take a crude joke without breaking stride. That, and I love to ski. Outdoorsmen have a very specific appeal to me; skiing with them is sort of like building up a callous. And that thickened skin protects you from nuisance—on and off the mountain. It exists for a reason, helps you move forward and do more.

I feel safe in groups of men. Or perhaps I should say that I feel safe in this group of men. They are mostly longtime friends and I have built trust and camaraderie one ski lap at a time, in backcountry bunk rooms, cabin kitchens, yurts, and skin tracks. There is no way that I would miss a backcountry ski trip with some of my favorite people just because I am the only girl. "Miss this?" I ask. I track the bottle as it circles the room and watch my friends reach for the booze, smile, laugh, and joke. Crow's feet spike from their smiling eyes. Most of the guys already have goggle tans and strong legs from early season skiing. I see the excitement in everyone's faces; we are all eager to begin our annual trip. We sit easily together, sprawled on chairs and beds, propped up against walls, hats pushed back on heads. The bottle is passed to me and the heat of the vodka feels good in my stomach. Outside the temperature dips, and the wind picks up.

∧ ∧ ∧

I grew up with boys. My older brother, Peter, is two years my senior. My younger brother, Jim, is two years younger. Sibling spacing remains a fact of life—I will always be between boys. In the rural expanses of New Hampshire, by some fluke, my closest neighbors were also boys. From an early age, I was surrounded. I became comfortable with men, in a way that eludes some women, simply because boys were a constant presence. I couldn't imagine a life without them. My parents dressed me in Peter's hand-me-downs. Corduroy, boy jackets and pants, blues, reds, browns, faded cotton plaid. Peter's life hung loosely from my shoulders and hips. I wonder if wearing someone else's clothing so consistently can change you, if I absorbed some of my brother through his duds. I followed Peter in his interests and experiences and that guided my childhood—I became a pitcher for our local Little League baseball team and learned to dribble a gritty basketball on a makeshift court.

On the edge of the White Mountains, where the lake nestles into the forest, our childhood unfolded. The dirt road that snakes by our home has potholes in the summer and frost heaves in the colder months. My dad made a parking space into a basketball court, and we played baseball with the local boys in a neighborhood field. We were four miles from the nearest small town with the mailing address of RR2, which stood for Rural Route 2. When my hair was still so blonde it was almost white, that was the first address I memorized.

The three of us grew up on the hiking trails of the White Mountains. Each kid had sturdy leather boots flecked with leaves and dirt, the treads worn, the metal eyelets punctuating shiny tracks where a parent repeatedly pulled laces tight. We did most of the hikes as a family, our parents bribing us to leave the lakeside in the morning. Other times we were scooped up from the babysitters to go on "dinner hikes" to eat cheese and bread on an accessible rock outcropping with a view. My mother was the ultimate facilitator, pushing lunch deep into her pack, dressing us in the warm layers demanded by a crisp fall day. She seemed content to let my father lug and lead us up mountains.

Early on, Jim rode in the backpack fast asleep on the way up the sides of the peaks, his curly blond hair lapping at the faded backpack, his chubby calves swinging with each of my father's steps. I gripped my dad's hand on the way up the trail, thinking that he could help drag me up the steep parts, help me keep up. Often, my dad crossed a stream three times to shuttle each kid over the moving water. I locked my arms around his neck as he moved from one exposed rock to the next, bearing me steadily across the watery vein. On each knobby peak in the White Mountains we sat on the lichen-etched rocks and ate gorp, looking out into the green wilderness of New Hampshire.

Sometimes the Canada jays swooped down to pluck food from

our hands, mittens forgotten in the glee of watching the birds' wings spread and curl. Their fine, long, gray feathers batted the air with each launch from a nearby tree. My brothers and I would offer up innumerable morsels to their greedy beaks, marveling at their scratchy, jointed feet.

Winters brought a snowy lake surface that called forth skis, skates, sleds, and snowshoes. Fat snowflakes sifted down to cover the frozen oval, and duckbilled, blue cross-country boots emerged. Sometimes we crammed onto a toboggan so Dad or Mom could drag us across the quiet expanse. The best was being whipped around in a circle and leaning against centrifugal force until they would let go of the rope and we would spill onto the lake in a pile.

My dad punched holes in the gray-black ice with his axe to check the thickness before announcing that it was sturdy enough for play. Often, in the first blooms of winter, the ice is thin and clear. Belly down, my brothers and I would push our faces against the cold surface and looked past the bubbles and into the heart of the lake—silent and clear below its new glaze. Our noses prickled with cold as we huddled over the fresh ice. I wore hockey skates and didn't know until years later when my aunt got a pair of figure skates that there was any other choice. By the time I understood the difference, the metal claw at the front of the figure skate would trip me. I learned to love the hockey stop, the one continuous blade, the skates like all the boys had.

Days when the ice was clear, we would skate around the lake or break out a bed sheet to sail across the ice using only skates, the wind, and outstretched arms. The idea of winter winds dragging us across the lake always sounded better than the reality. The cold breeze would whip the sheet out of our hands or press it against our child bodies. We were never the same height to create equal masts. Rarely did we understand how to best position short arms and the sheet to be swept forward. Magically, though, and only on occasion, the wind filled the faded sheet Mom had provided and scooted us across the ice, our blades rattling and shouts of joy bouncing off the hard surfaces. We couldn't see where we were going, as the sheet blocked our view, but it didn't matter because we were enthralled by the motion, propelled by the wind. These brief moments of "sailing" kept us chasing the wind across the ice until we were chilled and returned to the house with the battered sheet tucked up under one arm, craving the warmth of our wood-heated home.

We tended the skating rink in front of our house all winter, shovels pushing back the snow in long strips to keep the rectangle clear. The edges of the rink always curled at the sides, snowbanks providing a small barrier between rink and lake. The dock, frozen into the icy surface, served as one of the borders as well. As soon as each of us could walk, we were taught to push the old, battered red stool along the bumpy surface of the ice. And before long, we grew independent on our blades.

One afternoon while we were knocking a hockey puck around, Peter wound up for a slap shot. The noise of the stick scraped the ice and the slam of the puck cracked out over the lake. I took the puck in the neck—one of the only spots that wasn't muffled by winter gear. I went down. Usually, I would scramble onto my knees and then push myself onto my blades until I was vertical again. To save face, continue the game, and become tough like the boys, I would power through the bumps, the tears, or the pain. But this time, lying on my back on the ice, I felt the cold spread over my frame. With my view of the sky warped by tears, Peter and Jim skated into sight above me. They looked down on me and then at each other. "Should we get Mom?"

It was the silence that eventually prompted Peter and Jim to move toward the house and call for our mother. I don't remember my mom coming out, although I am sure she did. What I remember was the look of concern and surprise on my brothers' faces after I was hit by the puck. That, and the assurance that they knew almost instinctually how to move across the cold, hard skim of the lake to go get help.

∧ ∧ ∧

In the stirring cold of the helicopter pad, our group organizes boxes of supplies and ski gear. The boys and I hustle around the hanger in ski boots and down jackets. It takes four helicopter flights to get all twelve of us into the British Columbia backcountry. In Kokanee Glacier Chalet, I set up my sleeping bag in a cubby for "quiet sleepers." Brett is across from me, and Chris makes his bed on the top bunk above Brett. There are group divisions. Who snores. Who makes a strong cocktail. Who is ready to break trail and set the skin track. None of these lines break on gender.

In the mornings I wake early to appreciate the young light, check the weather, and get coffee before the rest of the lodge stirs, though there are other morning people. Slack and I lean against the big wooden beams and watch the snow fall as the light tips over the mountains. We make lunch and get ready for a day of skinning in a line toward our goal, and then skiing, one at a time, down a slope filled with powder, tension, and a scattering of trees. We motivate for that singular feeling of skis floating through snow. Each time someone skis, we have "eyes on." We say, "I've got ya," before a skier aligns with gravity. Then we track them carefully downslope so that if anything happens, we know exactly where they were.

One evening midweek, Chris makes Irish car bombs for the nightly cocktail. Having only two shot glasses, he makes only two drinks at a time. The drinking quickly evolves into races and then to grudge matches. Travis challenges me. After a few drinks already, heat flushes my face and I feel the buzz of the liquor. I move across the living room on tired legs to join him. Travis flips his shirt up to create a sort of a man bra, and I do the same. We literally belly up to the table and watch Chris make our drinks. We clink glasses and chug. A whoop goes up from the boys as I slam my glass down first. With this, I know I am done for the night, but also that there is no separation from me and the group. I'm just another one of the boys. Perhaps this is a tired cliché, and a ridiculous thing to celebrate, but it feels good.

I revel in the ease and the humor of these men, the drinking games and lewd comments, the push every morning to get out the door and into the mountains.

The next morning cracks early and claggy. The low visibility provides a perfect excuse for our slow start. White pillows of moisture cling to the valleys and float over the peaks. I follow the skin track methodically as we gain elevation, watching the back of the skis in front of me. Ahead, one of the boys pushes through the blank snow to create the track, pole marks dotting the sides. I slowly unzip my jackets and eventually take my hat off as I warm against the hill. Just in time for our first ski shot, the sun burns off some of the deep Canadian fog. We back off from one sketchy slope and pick a shorter, steeper line from a corniced ridge. We identify a no-fall zone and ski one-by-one down the mountain gullet. My legs again feel strong and ready for the day. I find myself in the middle of the pack, choosing my line and pointing my ski tips toward the clean snow next to the shadowed tracks of my companions. I hear, "I got ya," before I sink into my first turn.

∧ ∧ ∧

One spring during college, most likely 2002, my brothers and I found ourselves in Tuckerman's Ravine on Mount Washington with our cousin, Nic, and friends Silas and Saben. We were locked into a steep bootpack up Right Gully. Above and below us a long line of steps plugged into the snow slope. Our only option was up, and Peter led our group step by step toward the top. The bootpack, icy from compression and use, demanded attention. I set my feet carefully, my knees bumping against the slope. We worked up the vertical wall. I stared at the snow, my next step, or the slow crawl of the guy in front of me. There was no changing position, passing, or falling behind. These boys of my childhood had turned into mountain men; it was an easy evolution.

My childhood provided training, including bumped knees, launching into cold water, baiting hooks, and trying to keep up. It seemed natural to find myself working up an icy staircase with my brothers. Peter remained the leader, the technical student of mountains. Jim more often played support for me. I was in the middle: this was inscribed all over our past and future. I thought about our names in a line, too. Somewhere in the main building on the campus of The White Mountain School is a dusty award. With an old ice axe and ancient piton rides the title "Mountaineering Award"—perhaps the most coveted annual plaque the school gives at graduation. My name is sandwiched between my brothers' names, a few years apart. In a long list of boys, my name on that metal and wood award always made me proud.

I planted my shortened ski poles firmly before each step, trying not to glance down to the long sweep of ravine below. If I pulled from the bootpack, I would most likely take the guys behind me down, too. The same was true for the boys ahead of me, forming a chain of trust. I slammed each foot into place. Above me, outlined in the light beyond the ridge, Peter swiveled to holler at us.

"If you were clients, I'd have you roped!"

No one responded, and we continued up. I trusted Peter. He was an accomplished mountain guide and I felt safe following in his footsteps. The fact that a smile rode his face and he continued to push us upward felt expected, comfortable even. Ski pants whispered with each step, and I felt my toes protest against the front of my boot every time I kicked into the slope. From the front of the line Peter could see our skis and snowboards strapped to our packs, our bodies tilted to the hill, our willingness to move against gravity, to follow him.

By this time, Jim had surpassed me in size and ski skill. I relied on him as much, if not more, than on Peter. His words often bent with encouragement. In general, despite being older, I was content to follow behind him, knowing the duckbills of his tele boots flexed in the same way mine did. At times Peter moved out of earshot, whereas Jim reacted to my pace, slowing his own to maintain a verbal and visual connection.

That day in the corn ramps of Tuckerman's Ravine, we took four laps. This was three more than most of the other parties in the bowl. This may be because the skiing was good, or the glee was contagious, or because we were there and we could. Stopping for lunch, we claimed a wide, flat rock among the "lunch rocks" jumbled at the bottom of the ravine. The dark granite had absorbed the sun all day, and the warmth was welcome. Peeling off ski layers, we dug out chocolate and cheese, bread, gorp, and sandwiches. The sun flushed our cheeks. Together, we laughed more than we do when we are apart. Perhaps we lingered longer than usual, using the amphitheater of Tuckerman's Ravine to magnify our happiness.

Eventually, we stowed food and drink and headed out for our final lap on Hillman's Highway. As we left the lunch rocks, my quads already felt spent, responding to the steep steps and the lunges of telemark turns from the first three laps. The group buoyed my tired body, and the desire to keep up helped to motivate me up the hill. I found out later on the car ride home that although my legs were tired, they weren't flashing with cramps the way Nic's were. He cried out in the passenger seat as his legs seized up. We pulled off the road, car askew, next to a snowy field. We unloaded onto the gritty roadside to stretch our sore muscles, the jokes and tired quads quietly pulling us home after another long day in the backcountry.

^ ^ ^

Each morning in British Columbia, we disperse through the sprawl of the Kokanee wilderness. It's safer to travel in smaller groups, and this gives people terrain options. The afternoon of the last day of the trip, our split groups inadvertently meet up on one summit. All twelve of us stare into the distance at the big mountains that surround us. On many flanks and visible ramps of snow, our tracks linger as evidence of the week of powder hustling. The snow has started to sink with heat and roller balls leave long trails on south-facing terrain. I sip hot chai tea from an offered thermos. We weigh options. Some skiers look down the steeper, north-facing terrain into a snowy gully for their last run.

I opt for a sun-beaten slope because I feel confident about the stability. Our group watches half of our friends cut deep turns in the steeper run. I'm happy to see them disappear down over the roll and into what I assume is more powder. Once they are out of sight, the rest of us move off together to carve through trees and heavier snow. We whoop with the joy of the fall line and leapfrog downward. My partner and I work downhill with eyes on each other and ears open for other group instruction. I think about my brothers and how much they would love to carve turns in these big-bodied mountains, how they would fit in with this group.

We gather again on the lake that marks the end of our run and stretch skins back onto our skis in the spill of the bowl. The other group, now on the far side of the mountain in a different drainage, will be transitioning as well. Coming from different directions, we all ski back toward the lodge.

Months after the trip is over, I reflect on the gender dynamics. But they are slippery for me. I honestly don't think about being the only girl—but other people certainly do. I want to just be a skier in a group of skiers. People keep asking me, "How was it?" I don't know what they are looking for, exactly, but I know I never give them the answer they want. "It was fine; we had a wonderful time." I end up detailing the warm lodge and nearby glacier, the evening games, and the turns and ridges instead of the conversations and interactions. My hopes—that indeed no one is thinking about gender, just about skiing and laughing and fun—are affirmed when I press the group to think on it. When I ask them how they felt about eleven men and one woman, Shawn's response is the most telling, and I love him for it: "Last year was all dudes, wasn't it?"

VERSIONS

1.

During the summer mornings of my childhood, my mom often practiced yoga on our dock. I can see her like a snapshot in my mind: yoga mat unrolled wide to the mountains, loons assaulting the silence with their prehistoric calls, sun sparkling off the ruffled lake, and the water plants pushing their green heads against the undulating surface. My mom would strike her poses: the Warrior, her body cutting the air, or she might choose Half Moon or Downward-Facing Dog. My mom spread her toes wide, leaned into her muscles, and flexed in the morning air. Her yoga practice represented how she cared for herself, as the rest of her day was spent carting kids around in the maroon Colt Vista, zipping coats and tying shoes, boiling water to mold mouth guards, packing lunches, and helping to type homework on the electric typewriter. I grew up with this woman twisting and arching through her poses, muscles caught taut around the routines of motherhood.

This version of my mom, the one that I know, has only existed for the last thirty years. I suppose it started when she left Los Angeles to move back East to a small town in the White Mountains, the town she grew up in. Nestled in the hills, she returned to a place with no grid pattern, few stoplights, and white church steeples that needle the air. A place where my father worked as a printer and her parents still lived up the street. She came back from California for her younger sister's wedding and then stayed. In the years since her return, her primary focus has been us—her three children. Now, with her hair steadily graying, we have moved away from the lakeshore and into rentals with roommates and taken jobs of our own. She calls and emails and talks—keeping up as much contact as we will allow.

In her professional life she teaches yoga, stringing poses together to create a class, to stimulate muscles or encourage relaxation. I picture her bending easily at the waist, splaying her toes, and instructing. Then, moving around the room to shift a student's weight, she will give a suggestion or say, "Beautiful." In her classes, I imagine a room paved with rubberized mats, conscious breathing, and her calm, encouraging voice. On occasion, I will paint her toenails some outrageous color like coral orange. In the late-day sun of a summer afternoon, I'll brush thick lines of lacquer onto her toes, knowing that she allows this more for me than for herself. I think of her in yoga classes with her bright toes, tiny flares in her otherwise serene classroom. I imagine these things because I have never been to one of her classes.

Maybe I would love the practice of yoga; I have no doubt that it would be the foil to the aggressive sports I pursue: running, hiking, paddling, skiing, and riding. I'm not sure why, but I wanted to stand apart from her in this way. Despite her constant invites to attend class, I always chose something else. Maybe it was my own, sad version of rebellion. On the occasion that I have tweaked my body, she gently offers a few stretches that may help, bending freely on our kitchen linoleum to illustrate how to elongate my seized muscles. I know it must hurt her that none of her children have ever taken a yoga class from her, but even knowing this I cannot bring myself to make the time. And in this way, it hurts us both.

I envision yoga as balancing, smooth, and satisfying. It has always been my mother's thing, though; it's how people in the community know her. Often, strangers tell me how calming my mom's voice is. That same low, comforting voice has spoken the lyrics of my life. She talks, she calls, she writes, she questions. But before she was my mother, she was something else entirely.

2.

When my mom graduated from the University of New Hampshire in the fall of 1971, she was romantically involved with an instructor there. I imagine him as severely intellectual, mysterious, and not from a rural place. I believe that his mind must have been alluring. Together, they moved to Los Angeles. He was headed to USC for graduate school in cinema, and she was headed anywhere but home. She joined him and they drove cross-country. They didn't take their time when they motored from the Atlantic to the Pacific, swapping one coastal outline for another. She says she would do it differently now; she'd see the breadth of the country. Perhaps she wanted to acquaint herself with all those states so different from New Hampshire, focus less on the miles to go until Los Angeles and more on the green canopies of New England, the patched agricultural guts of our midsection, the deep red creases of the Badlands. It could simply be that she didn't even know what she was missing during the drive, or that she didn't want to know what she was missing. Once on the edge of the West Coast, she settled into a place that represented the flip side of her upbringing.

I conjure my mother in Los Angeles, walking the unfamiliar streets and finding a place so removed from her childhood home that it all felt shiny and new. It was starkly different from the small town where she grew up—where her neighbors and classmates were the same people she went to church with, folks who shopped at her father's grocery. Her hometown must have felt small and expected— from the movie theatre to the ski hill—always recognizable faces. She says what she loved about Los Angeles was the anonymity of the city, of being unknown. I imagine eye makeup and boots; I imagine spunk, a flirt. Picturing her on a beach in a daring bikini, soaking up the heat against the sand, makes me smile. What I know is thin: she worked first in the print industry and then the fashion magazine world. She loved the Mexican food, hot pastrami sandwiches, and fish markets found on the city streets. At some point she broke up with her taxi-driving, screenplay-writing, grad-student, ex-teacher boyfriend. Moving to Hollywood, she claimed a bungalow of her own and dated a man almost old enough to be her father. She broke the Catholic rules of her childhood. She sipped scotch to fit in.

This woman, this girl, is captured for a moment in a series of photographs tucked away in an album, black and white snapshots of my mother in short skirts, wearing her bedroom eyes. Caught in poses of happiness under a big oak tree, she is clearly involved with the man behind the camera. You can see the connection in the way she looks into the lens, her dark eyes claiming the anchor and focus of the photos. Her hair, shocking in its body and luster, encroaches on her face. She looks confident in the photos, like she belongs there.

3.

I would like to have met the girl in these pictures. But where is that spicy young woman now? Where is the independence and courage that pushed her into the asphalt tangle and rush of LA? I yearn to know both versions of her. I wish that the transition had been a little more messy and a little less complete. How does someone go from boots and smog to bare feet and the quiet of a yoga studio?

I shouldn't be surprised at her deft slip from one life to another; it's an art I practice. I know how I do it. It's how I can sink into the comfort of my preppie side, how a dress that zips up the side can feel supportive, how the right size pearl is tasteful, how sometimes straight hair can benefit from straightening. Then I can march into a ski hut with ten men, wear dirty clothing for a week, sweat waves of salt onto my backpack, and laugh at the dirtiest jokes. It is a swing that is almost balancing; it's reassuring that I find comfort in multiple worlds.

My mom has shucked that city woman, and the people of LA who knew her at that time are gone. The record seems wiped clean; the clothing no longer waits for wear; the makeup dried and tossed; the scotch a desire forgotten. Perhaps it's the age difference that has made the LA fling seem so far away, a chasm that cannot be bridged between us. It must be the youth that makes the person I imagine unattainable; she seems so completely beneath the surface of my mother. A time intentionally buried. I feel like that woman, my mother's former self, would understand my life—my rootless search, my willingness to get in the car and drive.

4.

When I was twenty, in 2002, I drove across the country with my best friend, Amanda. It was the first time that I dared to point my car westward and drive it all the way. The first day on the road I drove from New Hampshire to Mt. Pleasant, Michigan, to pick up Amanda. I was piloting my new-to-me red, two-door, Pontiac GrandAm GT, the clutter of my summer ambitions settled in the trunk and back seat. In the middle of the night I realized that I was driving the wrong way down a one-way street. With no cell phone and no GPS, I pushed past my desire to give up; I pulled a U-turn and continued to search for Amanda's house.

On our way westward from Michigan, Amanda and I stopped to take pictures at those sweet invisible lines between states and time zones. It felt daring, like we were wild in the face of our upbringings. We had no furniture and no place to live. We were simply two girls who wanted to survive paycheck to paycheck. Amanda and I posed heroically near the car for photos while we pushed the accelerator all the way to Bend, Oregon. During that drive, in a small journal, we kept track of how many honks and waves we earned from our fellow highway navigators each day. It was summertime and we were ready to bare our legs and loose our hair. We were ready to be young and a little reckless, ready to escape the confines of an East Coast preppy college and the gaze of our parents.

Amanda and I exchanged all we knew to create fresh versions of ourselves. For work, we became wranglers, spending hours on end in heavy western saddles. Our required outfits included Wrangler jeans, button-down shirts, a cowboy hat, boots, and a belt with a buckle. Dressed in our western duds that quickly wore to the contours of our bodies, we flung ourselves into summer. We happily flaunted our small waists and long legs, donning our clothing like we were wearing costumes. During long lunch breaks, we would practice roping a fake steer head skewered into a hay bale. Or we'd nap in the shade of the big pine trees with our hats tipped over our eyes. In time, the outline of riding wore into the seat of our jeans, faded white arcs representing hours in the saddle. Dust worked into our lives in unimaginable ways, dirt highlighting our features, sand against our scalps, residue from long days on dry trails.

In the evenings, the cowboys would buy us Mike's Hard Cranberry Lemonade. That sugar-alcohol combination will forever bring me back to the cool desert nights of Bend. To this day, I don't understand how I drank so much of the stuff. We would search out rodeos and bull bashes, take the horses on a picnic, go swimming at area lakes. Country music became our new soundtrack, when Garth Brooks was king and Keith Urban just a rookie. We danced on flatbed trucks, our boots scuffing the metal pattern of the big rig. Late at night, we would play drunken croquet or pool. And in between, we shared a double blow-up mattress in a studio apartment, cleaned the carpet by scraping it with a foam flip-flop, and ate dinner off plastic plates perched on a footstool as we sat on the floor. It was cheap, and make-do, and perfect.

One night, we rallied one of the cowboy's trucks up a sand dune to watch a meteor shower. The cowboys, Amanda, and I sprawled in the cold metal pickup bed with our heads perched on bunched-up jackets to watch the streaky sky, marveling together. It almost felt like someone else's life. Amanda and I could lose ourselves in that summer. We could flirt with cowboys, wear short skirts and shamelessly tight jeans, because it all came with an expiration date. This was not how our lives would end up.

5.

I meet my mom for lunch. Once we settle behind bowls of soup and salad, I say, "I want you to tell me about your time in LA." We talk about the sequence of jobs that she went through, one she landed by flirting with men down the street. We talk about how she took a trip to Palm Springs. How the forest of softwoods, the elevation, and the clear, crisp air made her cry. The familiar outlines of mountains reminded her of home, a place that maybe she forgot she was still in love with. She says of the view and her tears, "It ambushed me." Riding the cable car to gain a mountain vista must have echoed of home. The tram car in Palm Springs, as I look at it online today, mirrors the aerial tram on Cannon Mountain, red and yellow cars that glide through the heart of New Hampshire's Franconia Notch. Sometimes, when I drive East, it is Franconia Notch that catches my breath. The mountains splitting in front of me, the gray face of Cannon Cliffs, the Franconia Ridge line. It's how I know I am home. Sometimes, before I get to the place where ski trails spill into Echo Lake, I am crying, too.

My mother's heart must be shaped like mine, an organ that resonates with the ideas of home despite her effort to leave the small town behind. She said that she loved her older boyfriend in LA, but that he wasn't someone to end with. Stepping out into the cold together after lunch, we stride across the street and she says, "I'm not sure why talking about LA makes me so sad. Maybe it's because I feel like at that time in my life I had no idea who I was." Thinking about this, and how I have chased different versions of myself all over the world, I can understand her frustration. Sometimes I move because I don't know who I am, and I am trying to discover what version of myself keeps resurfacing no matter where I go, because that must be the real one.

6.

My mom still does yoga on the dock during the summertime. Her body, though, has changed in the last five years. Her muscles have pulled away from her bones, leaving a drape in her once-toned physique. Her hair, now almost completely white, tops a frame that has lost the pounds that denote health. For the first time since I was an adult, we can share clothing, she can slip into a size four or six, find comfort in pants that ride my frame too tightly. We have fun trying on my dresses for upcoming weddings; the shades of my closet swing freely from her hips. Often in the afternoon sunlight of the deck, I zip her into old bridesmaids dresses, college cast-offs, and recent acquisitions. Smile lines and crow's feet crowd her skin, but still, she slips from one yoga pose to the next. The flexibility and precision of her positions persist; yoga seems to be the constant pillar of her days.

The changes I notice in my mother are not due to the distances that I have traveled. Sometimes you notice things when you have been away—but this reaches beyond the simple shifts of an aging parent. Long distance phone calls in the evenings speak to an invading illness. Mom has a chronic cough that is often worse at night. In the middle of the conversation the insuppressible cough will coil through the phone—I can tell when she tips the receiver away from her mouth and hacks. She says, "Hold on" or "Wait a minute," and then, "Sorry." The hardest thing is that I've become used to it, started to believe that it is part of her life now. That occasionally she will cough blood, that she won't swim to the rocks in the middle of the lake with me, that when I call midday she may be resting. It's nothing I ever wanted to witness.

Her chronic illness has chased her for the last six years. It is a combination of allergies and bronchiectasis. How long can a family hope for wellness? The sickness changed the woman that I have known my whole life. It's like a delicate shell is left, one that still holds all of the love and wit of her core, but lacks the sturdy nature of her younger self. Once more a version removed from the college graduate in LA. I documented this woman, the mother who now coughs and rests. I detailed her struggle in a letter to the disability office. What I should really do is show them the vibrant woman in the LA photos smiling in the sun.

7.

For the seventh year in a row, I am moving to the West Coast after a summer of working in New Hampshire. It's 2013 and my fall pilgrimage seems nearly inevitable. Afraid of feeling confined in the familiar landmarks of my childhood, my life is caught on repeat. My departure has been planned for a while, my hopes carefully piled into a new location. I'll try Bend, Oregon, for a winter. Bend hasn't been the place where I rent and grocery shop since that summer with Amanda eleven years earlier. Maybe this time I'll stay. While my father and I strategically pack my dented Subaru, my mother measures flour, cardamom, and sour cream. She stirs, sifts, folds, scoops, and fills our home with good smells. Cake and cookies puff in the oven, dirty bowls and spatulas crowd the sink. This is one of the ways she says goodbye, over and over again: she bakes goods for my drive. The carefully packed Tupperware jiggles in my passenger seat all the way West. This is not the time for airy desserts, but dense coffee cake and peanut butter and chocolate chip cookies. She also spreads apples, dried fruit, and clementines on the table. Mom is helping me to stock up. Finally, the morning of my trip, she makes me a sandwich from leftovers. There is something inexpressibly sad about this for me, because I know she wants me to stay, but she continually helps me to go.

I like the woman my mother has become, but it still doesn't stop me from wanting to know the mystery of her past. I want to know how she bridged the gap between city and country, between flirt and marriage, between going and staying. I have something to learn from it. Maybe it had to do with my dad. He must have been the kind of guy to end with.

When she moved back from LA, she took a job at a publishing company where my dad worked in the print room. She had gained enough knowledge of the printing industry and layout to estimate how much it would take to put an idea on paper. She became a saleswoman. My mom's life intersected with my dad's in the thick colors of ink, when printers were still using the hot metal and wood blocks of the old letterpresses. With the whoosh of the newspaper press and the clacking of the bindery as a soundtrack, my dad worked with lead and zinc and paper amid the harsh smells of cleaners and ink.

One day, my dad and his brother offered my mom a ride home. She refused, saying that she preferred to walk. But eventually, she must have said yes. Maybe it was when my dad started to drive his soft, yellow, E-Type Jaguar in the summer months, or when he let his brother find another ride. Eventually, though, they came together. That was when she stayed.

As I drive away from home this time, warm tears slip down my mother's face. She and my dad stand together, waving. I just barely keep my own tears at bay, turning onto the main road with blurry vision. I practice this quelling almost every time I depart from the East Coast. In this moment, I can't understand why I am leaving the White Mountains. I will think about where I am going and where I come from for the next thirty-five hundred miles. As my belongings settle around me in the car, I greet the state lines, the traffic, fog, rain, and snow. Eventually tumbleweeds catch temporarily on my grill before dislodging. Often, I reach for a taste of home, packed with love, riding shotgun all the way West. I continuously watch the tiny digital display on my GPS count down the hours until I will arrive.

INTO THE BITE

I ask the owner of the ranch why nobody rides Belle. That isn't exactly right; Bud rides her occasionally. I have noticed this zebra dun mare in the packed dirt paddock. With her blond coat, she stands out amid the bays and flea-bitten grays. We pass her over as we collect horses for the string. Around her we grab horses with names like June, Billy Bob, Star, and Junior. She seems too delicate and pretty among this crew, and somehow left out. Belle stamps the flies from her legs, creating puffs of dust around her hooves, and watches as we gather the others.

Brooke, the owner, tells me I can ride her if I can get on her. I am drawn as much to the challenge as to Belle's demeanor, as if she is waiting for me. Perhaps I gravitate toward loners, outsiders that are set apart from the herd. And she is pretty in the way that sometimes veils danger. Her blond body fades to darker brown legs. As usual, I say yes. I say yes when I can. I want, somehow, to be set apart as well.

I saddle Belle up one afternoon in the late heat of the summer. Oregon buzzes around me. The Deschutes National Forest yawns, dust settling between the big trees. The river pushes its way through the desert. Coyotes and rattlesnakes avoid one another in the swelter. On the ranch, the big metal water trough collects a layer of scum. I brush Belle methodically. She seems almost bored with me, letting the brush move down her dark legs. Dust flicks off the bristles and is caught in the sunlight. I swing the heavy western saddle into place, settling the weight onto Belle's withers. I snug the girth carefully behind her front legs. I give the horn a few tugs to make sure the saddle is secure.

Slipping the bit into her mouth and tightening the throat latch, I lead her out into the arena. The bit pulls gently at her gray, velvety lips, causing a few delicate wrinkles to stack. Sun glints off the metal stalls and I move around to the fenced area. I notice that people have gathered. Brooke and her husband, Chuck, as well as my best friend, Amanda, and Bud and Brian all lean against the fence, arms folded over the top rail. They are in their western garb and the whole scene feels simultaneously authentic and fake. Amanda's straw cowboy hat shades her face, and her Wranglers are tight. She has one boot propped on the lowest fence rail like she was born to this life instead of having grown up in Michigan and attended college at a small, preppy, liberal arts school in the East. Amanda seems relaxed in the dust, between the men, bearing witness. It is clear that they are waiting to see what happens.

^ ^ ^

Aster was the first horse I ever fell off. We were cantering down a grassy hill, an awkward endeavor at best, and she bucked just once to toss me from the saddle. The distance between her broad back and the ground seemed infinite. I hit, rolled, stood, and brushed the dirt off. Tears welled in my eyes but didn't spill over. I was eleven.

Nearby, Aster cropped grass while the reins hung around her neck as if nothing had happened. I led her to the hill where I had fallen. Standing on the uphill side of her, I twisted my fingers into her dark, stiff mane and placed my dirty foot back in the shiny bell of the stirrup, hauling myself into the saddle. I can't remember now if I was afraid or angry. The important part was that I got back on. I knew, even then, that many little girls never rode after their first tumble from the back of a horse. Part of me, I imagine, was relieved. I had passed some sort of test. I clung to that action as a harbinger of the rest of my riding career. It's not that I was afraid of the fall—you almost never see it coming. It was the fear that I would stay down, or worse yet, never get on in the first place.

^ ^ ^

I swing Belle so that she is facing the crowd and away from the paddock's exit. This way she feels more confined; there is nowhere for her to go. She waits calmly as I cinch the girth again. These are practiced steps, and we are both patient. Finally, I flip the reins over her head and they fall loosely against her blonde mane. I sidle up and place one hand on her neck and clasp the rough leather slips of the reins. Here I pause and think about all the times I have swung into a saddle, how I have chosen Belle, how I have already said yes.

I lift my left boot up to mount. Immediately, as I place my toe into the stirrup, Belle spins hard into me. I move into the attack. I bounce twice on my right leg to catch up, push into the turmoil, and then launch into the saddle. It's an ugly way to get on a horse.

Once I am safely in the big seat, Belle stands still in the stirred-up heat and dirt. That's it. She spins when you mount up, answering the call of motion when boot hits stirrup. But Belle is not the first to teach me this lesson. If I had hesitated, I could have been stomped on, backed off, or exhausted. The trick is, when you say yes, you go.

Early training dictates a horse's ground manners. Horses learn to stand still, and this basic principle of horsemanship transfers to all the other safety aspects. The first and most important lesson is that the horse will stop. Belle lacked this command from the moment a rider tried to mount. The concern was simple. If you couldn't get her to stand still in the beginning, how could you expect that she would ever quiet? One disregarded command usually leads to another. And although it became clear to me that this was her main hang-up, she had been labeled as dangerous. She wasn't trusted, and when people become afraid of an animal, they transmit that fear into their own actions. Perhaps she amplified their anxiety too much, feeling their trepidation as soon as they moved in to mount. It's counterintuitive to get on a horse that is spinning, to close the gap between human and moving animal. Every horse is an individual, as is every horse-woman. Sometimes it's easier to understand the warnings than identify the solution. For me, pushing through the swirl of hooves and dust, curling my fingers into her coarse, oily mane, and choosing to join her felt instinctive. Once in the saddle, after passing her test, the rewards were immediate. I found myself squarely seated on a willing, honest animal. We had disproved those who had gathered for a different sort of display; they'd expected an unraveling instead of a coming together. She didn't scare me nearly as much as she interested me.

I spent my whole life learning from cast-off horses, animals that others were afraid of or didn't have time for. Belle was another project to learn from, and I felt like we were underdogs together.

∧ ∧ ∧

I started taking horseback riding lessons when I was five. Riding became sewn into my identity, each puncture and pull of the thread cinching the life of the big animals closer to my core. In junior high I rode with a family, the Scotts, in my New Hampshire hometown. The Scotts had a daughter named Käthe who was falling out of love with horses. They had two at the time, and I was picked up as a riding part-ner. I was basically given a horse to ride and the freedom to claim it. Käthe and I would take off with Aster and Tuckerman and do some of the most dangerous things I have ever done. I loved not knowing the risk and the abandon that comes with that. It seems like a property that can only belong to childhood.

After crossing a river and a broken concrete dam, Käthe and I would emerge at the corner of a field. With thick trees anchored by stone walls on either side, the massive field was always deserted, save for an occasional deer and, once, a black bear. This forty-acre field was mostly flat with a hill in one corner and a small, sunken pond in the center. In deep summer, the grass was high enough to brush our feet in the stirrups. Käthe and I would look at each other and then begin racing. We would mimic jockeys, pushing our bodies out of the saddle and letting our arms extend and recoil with each lunge of the gallop. Standing in the stirrups, it was pure bliss on a summer day, reckless and intoxicating. Aster's mane would whip up and down with her stride. We would reach the other end of the field breathless and happy, never once having thought of the potholes and hummocks in an untended field. Instead, the spires of the town church down below, the tall hay grass swiping past our feet, and the smell and feel of a galloping horse shaped the contours of our summers. Aster was never mine, but out on the trail especially, she felt that way.

In winter we were set loose on the snowy expanses of northern New Hampshire. Snowmobilers cursed us as we let our horses punch big holes into every trail we could access. Each stuttered step marked our path through the woods. We rode bareback to keep warm in the clear, cold months. Sometimes after a big storm we would jump off the horses and into the snow or gallop through the blanketed fields. Falling off seemed less daunting if we landed in the snow, no stirrups to tangle our legs. We continued our fearless escapades with few adults knowing the extent of our liberties, how brazen little girls can be on big animals.

Now I imagine horses sinking a fast leg into a groundhog hole, or both animal and rider cartwheeling over a hidden lump, a trip, or a snag, a slip on the ice or snow. Now I know that these were not my animals to risk with running. This ignorance, though, shaped me. I miss not knowing. All that time as a child on horseback eased the lines between animal and rider. During summer trail rides, I could feel the sweat of the horse seep through my jeans to sting my calves. After a long gallop we would come to a standstill and let the horses breathe, feeling the whole-body expansion of their hungry lungs, their big hearts pounding, reverberating through our saddles, hands, and legs. These moments stack and become thick with experience, leaving me confident and at peace in a saddle. I am part of an action and reaction; I am in relationship somewhere between instinct and training.

^ ^ ^

In my experience, there exist two types of horsewomen. The first type gets scared and turns timid or tense in her riding. She conveys this hesitation and fear directly to her mounts, fights the burden of being afraid, and then broadcasts it. There is no hiding from a horse. The other type gets angry. If a horse runs away with her, bucks her off, offers up a dirty stop, she gets pissed. I fall solidly into the latter category. In my later years as a rider for the St. Lawrence University equestrian team, I was often put on the horses that had run away with a beginner. I rode the new arrival or the wildcard. Through the neatly swept aisle of Elsa Gunnison Riding Arena I would hear my coach ask, "Cate, do you still have your boots on?" This always indicated that she wanted me to get on a horse already under saddle in the ring. For whatever reason, the horse needed something that I could give. I would plod into the middle of the dusty oval and mount up.

Once it happened when a sensitive Thoroughbred, Devon, ran away with our walk-trot rider. I got on, determined to put him to work. And through my seat and hands he could feel that I wasn't afraid, and that running would just be a lot of hard work for little gain. Another time I cantered a rehab horse, Daniel, for the first time in months. He let a string of monster bucks loose in his love of movement. My coach said she thought it was a fair fight, and I stood in the stirrups and let Daniel coil and spring with abandon. And then there was the new horse, Ria, who reared and bucked on the lunge line until my coach told me to get on. "Cowboy up, Cate," she ordered.

Instincts tell a horse to move into pressure. In the wild, this makes sense, to move into the attack or bite. Imagine the hunt—a herd of horses rumbling through dry terrain and bolting from a pack of wolves. Experience and death have taught horses that if a wolf or big cat attacks, they have a better chance if they move toward the teeth. If the horse moves away from the animals, the bite tears a hole in their bellies, necks, guts. Puncture wounds are better than open ones, so to keep their hides intact, horses learn not to pull away from an attack.

Moving into the attack seems reasonable to me. There is something innately satisfying about confronting the teeth.

^ ^ ^

Käthe and her family moved away. The strands of electric fence were cleared from their fields. The barns sat empty. I felt like a part of my childhood moved away when the Scott family left. I met a new woman, Deb, and her two horses. The first time I rode at Deb's house, I fell off, sliding into the lawn while people watched. I got back on. I wanted to be part of the motion. I wanted to ride the same trails that Käthe and I had galloped, to see if the horizon looked different from another animal. After the tough start, I ended up riding and loving an Egyptian Arabian named Zarruk. He was mean, but he was as close to being my horse as any animal before. Perhaps he was closer to my heart, too, because when he laid his ears back or lunged with his teeth bared, it made me more determined. The fact that he scared other people only pushed me closer to him, feeling, somehow, that we were kindred. Again, I said yes to an animal that was set apart by his actions, but also by his raw athleticism and his ability to fight me, and teach me as well.

Deb wrote into her will that Zarruk would come to me if anything happened to her. This both scared and shocked me. It felt more real than before. I went to college and still rode in the summers, turning Z loose up grassy hills and letting him run. He was pure fire, unpredictable and talented. I fell off of Zarruk more than any other horse I have ever ridden. But he also taught me more about staying on a horse than any other animal.

Zarruk died while I was abroad teaching in Switzerland. His death came the same week a student of mine died. The loss seemed too much to bear, and I couldn't tell anyone that this horse that was almost mine, this big, difficult, breathing animal that I grew up with and loved was being bulldozed into a field. The sadness over the student's death was already so much, my own grief already too great, and the campus so full of mourning that I couldn't add something that might pale in comparison. It felt selfish. Zarruk never deserved to pale next to anything.

∧ ∧ ∧

In the high desert landscape of Central Oregon, with volcanoes propping up the sky on the horizon, I fell into a summer rhythm that smelled of horses, leather, and pine. Belle became one of my wrangler horses for the rest of the summer. I learned to put my foot in the stirrup and mount, no hesitation, no spinning. I learned to trust her. I trusted myself. She turned out to be one of the most fun horses I have ever ridden. No one else rode her that summer after I tapped her as my mount. On days off, Amanda would take her project horse, Sandpiper, and I would take Belle, and we would ride out into the dusty foothills along the Deschutes River.

We would race, and even when I held Belle up to give Amanda and Sandpiper a head start, we flew past them every time. I like to think that Belle was pleased to be ridden, to move into shape, to have the attention. When I pushed my hand forward and let Belle have her head as we galloped full bore toward Amanda, I would feel that instant where everything was in motion, when all four of her feet were off the ground. That singular airborne moment renewed my trust in her each time, the big trees streaming past, the path of dust curling up behind us, the sweat rising to my temples.

When I left Oregon, Chuck tried to give Belle to me. But I couldn't cart a horse across the country. It was beyond my means. I wasn't a western rider. I had no barn. I had no money. I was twenty. That summer only held a temporary grip on the rest of my life. It saddened me that she was worthless to them, that no one else would ride her, that she was labeled flawed. With so many other horses that seemed saner, the perceived dangers of an unpredictable mount proved too much.

Someone had taught her long ago to spin, to duck her head and lean into the rider as a pivot point. I had simply noticed her in the dusty paddock, set apart by her idle beauty, and I wanted to take a chance on her. She loved me for the attention, for pushing through one bad action to redeem the rest of her. People who shied away from her habit missed out, and I was rewarded for seeking the challenge, for asking about her, for confronting the teeth.

THE WEIGHT OF HEALING

After the avalanche, the school, routine falters. I show up for my classes, but stop teaching. Students arrive, preoccupied with grief, if they arrive at all. Rita, the fourteen-year-old girl who died, is everywhere. The weight of the accident heaps in the silence of bookshelves, corners, and our imaginations—pressing in hallways, stairwells, and classrooms all at once. The sunshine betrays us with its radiance as we grapple with the ideas of "after."

James watched from above as the slope gave way. Before the accident he was one of the students in my class, but now he is also a witness. James skied the hard debris to the nearest lift, his edges cutting into the fast forming crust, fear his only companion. The German words for help, *Hilfe*, and avalanche, *Lavine*, heavy in his head. James avoids my eyes in class and I wait; I can tell he needs to say something. After all, he is the only one of us who was there. The whole class founders in these speechless moments. Sitting on the edge of his chair, he rocks his weight forward. Finally, he looks at his hands and says, "You just can't imagine how helpless I felt. You just can't."

No one speaks. He picks a small green square from the floor and starts to fold. For a week all we have done is make paper cranes during class. Sitting in a circle we spread the bright rectangles of origami paper on the scuffed floor. Almost fluorescent, the hot pinks and greens flare in the warm wooden room. First, we reduce them to squares and then crease them carefully into little birds. The sounds of folding scratch at the silence. I focus on the task of creating a figure from flatness. My fingers slip over the dry shapes, and white seams appear as we manipulate the paper. These cranes are all angles, and at the beginning of each class I have to pay attention to every careful fold. But the birds emerge more easily each time.

Nothing can bring Rita back. The cranes are for us, the survivors. One thousand of them, strung together, are supposed to speed recovery, bring luck, grant a wish. So, for James, for the students stunned in grief, for teachers who are lost, we fold. Between the library stacks, with the long glass windows and the toothy alpen vista at our back, we fold. And at the end of the period we perch the tiny birds in our hands, feel the slightest weight of progress.

HERD ANIMALS

It's 2009 and I've just finished graduate school and I am free, not tied to a particular person or place, once again chasing my ski tips through the mountains of the world. Las Leñas, Argentina, flowers in front of us. We enter the snow-laden peaks and leave the gritty snake of road behind. Around the shoulder of the mountain, tourists stand in line for the ski lifts. Crowds herd to popular trails. Droves of goggled people slip down the wide groomers. They reassemble in the sunny bars and restaurants strewn across the resort to eat and laugh together.

Chris and I embrace the isolation of the ridge, avoiding the masses tucked away from view. The Andes spread before us and our minds and bodies swell with the urge to explore the untracked. We point our skis away from the expected.

The flanks of the mountains overlap in deep rows of landscape. We skin toward the peak we have chosen and a bowl in the distance. The deep gut of the feature leads to the waiting pinnacles and gullies. By ten o'clock the sun bathes us from all directions, bouncing from sky to slope to body and back. After an easy hour we reach the steeps, and Chris sets a skin track up and away from me. As I stoop to open my side-zips and let the wind sweep my legs, I see Chris moving methodically higher. We leave the browning valley below and trek into the soft spring snowpack and shadowy powder of the mountains.

I don't need a mirror to know that my face is red, and that crusty lines of salt trace down from my nose and temples to gather at my chin. I push myself to keep up. Silence fills the surroundings as my skins bite into the sun-softened snow and crisp shadows. We gain thousands of feet. For a moment I am distracted, knowing that around the corner, out of eyesight, people crowd lifts and shops. They buy dulce de leche and salami, music pumps through outdoor bars, tourists sit to eat at long tables, and carafes of wine stand like beacons between them. I am outside all this with only the beat of my heart keeping time, the mountains and the movement sustaining me. Chasing my partner in adventure, I move against the weight of gravity toward the thrill of isolation and sport. Chris widens the gap between us and I refocus on each stride to shrink the space. Keeping him in sight is crucial; he is the only person out here with me. I move mindfully away from the masses, trying always to remember my way back.

^ ^ ^

Chris is my backcountry ski partner, and we have been traveling the mountains of Patagonia together for a week. It is this love of skiing in the blank pages of the mountains that binds us as companions. These things are understood between Chris and me: he is stronger and more knowledgeable than I am, he sets the skin tracks, and somehow, no matter my level of fitness, he always has legs for one more run. He planned the whole trip. His wife vacations in Spain while we hunt gullies and snow-filled bowls. Chris is angular and funny and has uncommon facial hair—a dash of stubble centered under his bottom lip. Around day four, I stop apologizing for my slowness; we have settled into travel together. Chris's face gathers sunshine in tones of dark brown; mine carries the sun in pink and red. People eye us with suspicion, a man and a woman traveling as friends and shunning the ski lifts in favor of *afuera del piste*. When one man offers to rent us a romantic villa, I reply, "We don't really do romantic." "Amigos," Chris says and we bump fists. Somehow the fist-bump has become our language to express friendship instead of romantic relationship. The man's expression twists. "Amigos?" he repeats, while panning a finger back and forth at us. "No funny business," Chris says. I smile politely, having become familiar with the reaction to our unconventional brand of camaraderie. I packed a gold band to slip on a finger and fake marriage if I needed to—just to make life easier as we navigated a more conservative culture. But the thick gold band that once belonged to my aunt stays behind the black mesh zippered compartment of my Dopp kit. I don't feel the need to circle the truth with a gold ring that would feel so unnatural on my naked finger anyhow.

∧ ∧ ∧

Now, as Chris climbs away from me, I watch him round corners and kick turns far above. I am left with the rush of the mountains, my breathing, and my own thoughts. I feel the warmth of the sun up the length of my body. This is where I am most fulfilled, following a track that stitches its way back into the bodies of snow-covered mountains. Skiing has been a soul pursuit for me, and I have chased this love all over the world. The glide of skis over snow and the pillowed falling of skiing in powder nourish me. The frozen isolation with the reward of turns and edges has become the place I feel most alive.

Above me on the slope, I see Chris pause on a small swale and look back to check my progress. I watch him dig for a camera as I climb to his vantage point. He points down into a sweet little bowl. Fingers of rock create a crown around the headwall. Not far away from us a single horse kicks through the crescents of wind-exposed rock searching for grass. Without proof, I immediately assume it is female: a little bay mare with a shock of white blazed up her face. She has angular hips and her ribs fan dangerously close to the skin. It's hard to tell if she is just old or close to death in other ways. The shaggy coat sweeps up and down with the wind as the small animal turns her haunches to the assault and stills. Her tail, pushed through her back legs, makes her hunched frame even smaller.

You don't have to know horses to know this is bad. A lone animal at eleven thousand feet has made a wrong turn. Horses are herd animals; she should be with a herd in the lower, warmer fields where vegetation still clings to the dry soil. A horse without a herd is left exposed and unprotected; separation from the others most often means death. I have known horses my whole life and feel deeply this animal's plight.

Chris moves cautiously until the horse's head swings our way and her ears prick in interest or fear. She heads straight for us. Chris tracks her progress nervously until he pauses to ask, "Will it come at me?"

"She shouldn't, but if she does, just face her. Square your body."

Chris moves on and the horse stops with a pillow of space between them. She is not yet desperate enough to close the gap and ask for help. At this point I feel the elevation, the extra suck of breath and wash of mind. I take her existence in with a few sweeps of my eyes. Knowing that this is not goodbye, and that we will ski to the bottom of the bowl and see her again, we leave her behind and ski upward to gain the ridge. We stand for only moments in the wind and absorb the mountains that cross, without markers, into Chile. We rip skins and Chris takes the first few turns to look down one of the chutes between two rock prongs. He disappears with a hoot, carried by gravity and skill. In this first run of the day, through the rocky stack of the Andes, he spills back into the bowl where the horse waits. The tired and hungry animal is lying down, head flat against the snow. It looks dead, a hulk on the corner of a rocky, exposed oval.

My turn to ski. I embrace the fall line momentarily and make short steep turns. Each arch mercifully slows my descent as the snow unfurls in front of me. My edges scrape down every turn, shedding a rain of snow around me. The horse lifts her head. Almost painfully, but perhaps this is only in my mind, her skeletal haunches move awkwardly upward in a heave to stand again. My skiing is disturbing the repose of a starving animal. My whole body catches with sorrow, a snag in my happiness.

Stopping at the bottom of the slope, I am out of breath and thrilled. Yet the image of the lonely horse rattles me; I'm uncomfortable so close to its destitution. She eyes us until we are again out of sight. We leave the isolated animal to the fading light and increasing winds. Our skis slide methodically over the deep snow and steep slopes. Each step upward adds to the turns we will eventually link to the valley floor.

Our last shot is over three thousand vertical feet of aching legs and heaving lungs. The turns fill me up as we wind back to the road that will take us to people and the smell of roasting foods. I snap pictures of the generous slopes and stunning mountains that circle us. And I wonder about the mare, hoping she can survive alone up there with only the knowledge that she has already come through the toughest months marooned in this beautiful harshness. I wanted to touch her, and I called out, but she didn't come because I had nothing to offer.

CLOSE

The first night we were both buzzed from the bar, it was three in the morning, and all we wanted to do was sleep. Sean had kept the small truck steady on the drive home, the headlights slicing the thick rural darkness, our eyes alert for movement. He said, "There is the couch downstairs, I can pull out the futon, or you can sleep in my bed."

"The bed would be the easiest," I explained. It's where I wanted to be, but I felt like I needed an excuse, had to justify my choice.

"That's fine," he replied.

I brushed my teeth in the little bathroom down the hall. With spearmint bubbles, I scrubbed away the steak and drinks of the night. I was weary from my long drive to the coast and the dinner and conversation that had stretched late. This circumstance was not unexpected, as we had known each other for a while, our lives intertwined through friends and family. I felt comfortable in the cubby of his bathroom and with the destination of his bed in mind. In the mirror I noticed the dilated pupils anchoring my blue eyes. I loosed my ponytail from the tie and watched my blond hair settle evenly against my shoulders. When I padded softly back to his room, the door was cracked and the lights were off. In the even darkness, I slipped into shorts and a tank top and crawled into bed next to him. The simple comforter was inviting, as was Sean's body, already warming the bed. I turned my back to him, and in one easy motion he scooped me into the curl of his body. His arms made me feel small and safe as they held me, his grip easing as his quiet snores soon circled in the night air. I relaxed into my own sleep and the sounds of his home.

In the morning, Sean was gone before I got up, off to guide rock climbing in town. His bedroom was sparse and quiet; the closet gaped open to reveal his leather jacket hanging heavily from the center of the bar and a few shoes scattered beneath. My small duffle was pushed up against the bureau and was the only clutter in the room. He lived in Otter Creek, Maine, just outside of Bar Harbor. There were reasons for me to be visiting this blue-eyed man. We had skied together in Switzerland the winter before in the company of my brothers. He was my older brother's friend. Sean's lifestyle had called to me then, his love of the mountains and the sunshine, his ability to pick up and ski for two weeks, his sweet ineptness in a foreign country.

An avalanche during that trip had buried his new skis, and he had never expected to see them again, which was easy to stomach considering what could have been lost. I had been working in Switzerland, so in the spring, I hiked to find the skis melted out of the snowpack, rusty edges the only sign of distress. I was visiting Maine, on a break from my teaching job, to surprise him with the reclaimed skis he had "left" in Europe. Excited to enjoy the national park Sean seasonally called home, I was also curious to see where our friendship would lead. I was waiting to discover if something more could accompany our easy laughter and flirty phone calls. Sean was tan from a summer on the rocks and strong from life in the mountains. His humor and fitness were alluring.

I spent my day running and hiking in Acadia National Park. Sean had left his park pass, a note, and a map to help me navigate the numerous trails. My skin was tanned, too, from spending days in the mountains; this was the first summer ever that I didn't have to work. I was twenty-four and I had the freedom to roam around and see friends, hike ridges, and wear out my running shoes. I trusted my body's strength, fitness, and tone that summer. It had never betrayed me.

When Sean came home, he changed into his jeans and leather jacket and we took his motorcycle out. His toothy smile flashed at me through the face shield of his helmet. I also donned my leather, an old brown jacket that was hand stitched in rawhide and pulled tight across my body. Wriggling into my jeans and grabbing my helmet, I was ready to tuck snug behind him, my long legs folded, feet resting on the foot pegs of his bike. Before we left, he reminded me to lean with him around the corners.

We sped up Cadillac Mountain to watch the sunset. To stay on the back of his bike, I hugged Sean's solid frame. My hands clung to his leather-clad sides, finding easy homes. I rested the edge of my helmet on his shoulder and smelled leather and pine. Occasionally, he would reach back and put a hand on my thigh as if to check that I was really there. On the way down the mountain, we coasted in neutral. The bike was silent as we carved the sharp turns. We went way too fast on the back roads, the tires spooling the pavement out behind us. I leaned into him and the corners as the wind and trees whipped by in blurry streaks.

Back at Sean's home, we went to bed. Again, he pulled me close against him. I lay awake listening to his deepening breaths as he drifted into sleep and I wondered why he was being so careful. Was it because I was his friend's little sister, or because he had just ended a long-term relationship? That night I heard the occasional car disturb the silence, the subtle breeze, and his heavy breathing beside me. The following morning, I let myself embrace the day's adventures and kept my mind occupied with the ocean views, my feet on the trail, and the direction of the wind. I moved steadily through the park, borne over rocky peaks and treed paths by my humming sneakers and the need to sweat. Mountains had always felt like home, so I sought the familiar instead of dwelling on the interpretation of the nights before.

The last night we spent together, nothing changed. Sean peeled back the covers of the blue-sheeted bed and pulled me into his warm, strong chest. His muscled arms held me close enough so I could feel his heart beat and his lungs expand and retreat. *There must be something wrong with me.* The thought nudged me all night long. The following morning was the only morning Sean didn't have to work, and we slept until thick lines of sunlight shot through the blinds. It was the day I had to get back to New Hampshire. He awoke and started to rub my back. "If you take this off," Sean said, pulling at my tank top, "I'll give you a massage."

Without much hesitation I pulled the pink stretchy camisole off. His tan hands worked my bare back in slow circles. He kneaded my shoulders. The room smelled like sleep. I pulled my sun-bleached hair to the side and enjoyed the attention. When the massage was done, I gathered my courage and turned to face him.

Sean glanced at me before sliding out of bed. "I'm gonna grab a shower," he said. He was out of bed before I could respond, leaving his bedroom door agape as he moved away. Stunned, I tried to focus my eyes, breathe. My body felt betrayed in its nakedness against his dark sheets in the morning light. Every bone in my body seemed unsettled and exposed, as if the framework of my person vibrated with the material of defeat. I didn't even want to cry; the situation didn't demand tears. All I wanted to do was move. I got up quickly and dressed while the sound of the shower hissed down the hall. I zipped on a purple hiking skirt and pulled a fresh tank top over my head, slipped my bare feet into sandals. Shaking a bit, I stowed the rest of my clothing in my duffel. I was ready to flee.

By the time Sean was out of the shower, I had my leather jacket slung over my shoulder and the helmet in my hands. "I'm all packed up," I said brightly as I moved past him and down the steps. I could smell his shampoo and feel the abating steam on his skin. "I want to get on the road early," I said over my shoulder. He was silent at the top of the stairs.

Sean ambled outside into the sunlight while I tossed my dirty, smelly running clothes into the trunk of my car. The sun made him squint as he said, "Thanks for coming up."

"Thanks for hosting me," I applied a smile. Sean hugged me before I ducked into my car. Gravel shot from beneath my tires as I drove too fast out of his driveway and away from where he stood, one hand cocked in a wave and the other shielding his eyes from the sunlight.

On the five-hour drive to New Hampshire, I cranked up the music to drown out the stories looping my mind. I guess I was a late bloomer, never having had a boyfriend before. I felt young and strange and sad, and movement felt like the right answer—I wanted to run. The open road home fed welcome mileage between me and my defeat. On the drive back, I tried to figure out how it had all gone so badly, thoughts spaced out in the silent moments between country songs. Anger and hurt settled in my gut. In time, I would tell myself a different version of the events, being more generous to both of us.

BEYOND THE VIEWFINDER

It's the winter of 2010 and I rejoice in my ability to pursue my ski dreams with friends; I know I am fortunate to have a great summer job and a flexible winter life. We have planned this trip on the cheap, splitting five ways a shitty minivan rental and three weeks in a finished basement with kitchenette in Anchorage. A sweet woman in town cooks us breakfast and dinner. These meals are a bit dubious— she is feeding us old salmon and whatever meat she can get us from her freezer or for free—but we eat them anyway. I might be eating old salmon and earning my turns, but I'm doing it in Alaska with the best people—this, to me, is the definition of good fortune.

On the grimy pavement of Thompson Pass in the throat of the Chugach Range in Alaska, with Lady Gaga pumping from the open doors of the minivan, we shove feet into ski boots and pull our layers on in the breeze. We don't start the day taking pictures; nothing about our preparation is worth capturing. I pass sunscreen around the group while rubbing the citrus-smelling grease onto my own face. This is our morning routine. With laces pulled tight, skins stretched onto the bottom of each ski, and beacons checked, we finally cross the road and climb the dirty snowbank. I toss my skis onto the crusted snowmobile track and stoop to clip my bindings into place. My toes fan coldly in my boots and I just want to get moving. These mornings hold the promise of the day to come, but are not the glory shots of any ski trip. This is the unrecorded labor of logistics.

We are headed for the "Berlin Wall," a popular destination not only for backcountry skiers, but also snowmobilers. A wide highway of tracks scar the gully up to the saddle. The morning light is young enough that we ski alone, in silence. The snowmobilers are still sleeping or having breakfast. Our group of five—four men and me—slips up the gully, keeping to the right of the machined tracks. My two brothers and Silas, Saben, and I work easily together in the morning chill to gain elevation. Our figures hunch forward in the practiced strides of skinning. Our faces already look chapped from the previous days out, goggle tans riding our cheekbones. Even this early, we do not smell good. Beneath our layers, beacons blink, our hearts pound, and tired ski clothes become damp with sweat against our bodies. Day packs weight our backs and shift with each kick turn. I stand out as the solo girl only because my clothing is colorful and my form slighter. The slope gently meets the glacier, and we keep our heads down as we make a slow zigzag up the skin track. My feet start to warm, and I keep up well with the group, working the approach before the steep alpine terrain begins.

We don't stop for pictures until we turn solidly away from the thoroughfare and onto the clean contours of the glacier. The white of sunshine reflects off the snow all around us. We gain toward a panorama of dark ridges finning the air and snowy runways that plunge down from jagged peaks. The scope overwhelms, as mountains stack in the background and fingers of snow sprawl from the highest points. Cornices hang expectantly in the sun and shadow of the day. We keep our eyes fixed on our destination and turn our backs to the road, power lines, and snowmobile tracks.

The whine of sleds begins to echo in the deep recesses of the mountains as we move steadily toward the col. Just as I am gaining the saddle, a snowmobile carrying guided clients roars past and parks on the flat break in the mountains. I am simultaneously envious and annoyed, but at the end of the day I will know how we made the ridge. My clothes will not be compromised by the lingering petroleum signature. The clients' guide lines them up for a photo. I attach my skis to my backpack and devour a peanut butter and jelly sandwich while I watch the careful orchestration of the scene. The four men in the group have the thick webbing of harnesses pulled up over their colorful Gore-Tex jackets. Their packs are puzzles of skis, straps, and poles. It all looks very technical. They hold up imposing ice picks like trophies of alpine dreams. Behind them spreads the Chugach Range in all the snow-filled glory of a skier's heaven. The men smile into the camera, their faces fresh and relaxed. Their guide captures this image, flattening one version of truth into the single dimension of sight. Cropped out of the frame are the heavy, dark bodies of the snowmobiles. The guide is also absent, removed by the lens. And any trepidation they might feel standing on the edge of a big mountain adventure is erased by the call of the photographer to lean closer and smile.

My thoughts turn inward as I watch these men pose for another shot: pictures lie. Or maybe it's just their orchestration. Photographers search for the best view, the highest peak needling the horizon. They force everyone closer to accommodate the viewfinder. They frame the surroundings to fit their desired representation, something worthy of hanging on a wall or propping on a coffee table after the trip. Listening for the subtle click of the shutter, we smile, no matter what we feel, turning toward friends or lovers we may be uncertain about. Grins flicker, saving the version that we believe people want to see, documenting what we want to remember in the future about the past.

I have become a keener critic of pictures on this trip because my brother Peter has packed in his heavy, professional camera. He came to Alaska to ski but also to capture shots he can sell to magazines. Peter is aware of brand names: the Black Diamond logo or the Patagonia patch. He searches for the emblematic and dramatic, for an image that sells. But it's different for me, as I hold my tiny silver point-and-shoot. I am looking to seize mementos that will trigger memories of the larger story of our trip, the story beyond the edges of the photograph.

After the boys and I finish our sandwiches, shove a few handfuls of gorp down, and take some long pulls from our water bottles, we are ready for the real business of the day. We make harnesses out of webbing—the three younger siblings watch carefully how to loop and tie. We are about to head up the Berlin Wall ridge. The terrain ahead demands attention, the alpine blade dropping away thousands of feet on either side. The guided skiers are already picking their way across the ridge, one at a time, tied to the guide who shuttles them over the exposed slice of mountain. Their figures look hunched and tentative, carefully placing their ice axes to spear confidence. The guide talks them through the exposure. We see their slow progress, the rope, and hear the occasional clang of metal on rock. Despite our harnesses, we do not rope up. We will be faster without the tether. The ridge seems negotiable, so our harnesses ride our hips in case we need them later. We crawl as a group across the exposed areas. Peter and Silas strategically place me in the middle, insulated by my brothers on either side. It is where I feel most comfortable, with Peter leading and advising ahead of me, and Jim supporting me a few steps behind. To the immediate right or the left of me, the intense sunlight illuminates the fall of the mountain, the deep relief of the valley, the consequences. Snow and rock calve away beneath the ridge and leave sharp, steep runways. I do my best to look forward instead of down. I notice my breathing.

"Look back over your shoulder and down the ridge," Peter says. Here, where the ridge still feels precipitous, he documents, asking me to look up or down while hiking. Peter, his face obscured by the bulky camera, seeks bright colors and a half-recognizable female face.

I appeal to him as a subject because of gender and circumstance. In addition to being his sister, and a passionate skier, I am unmistakably a woman—even the color of my gear cries female. I have Gore-Tex pants with a shiny flower design, a light blue jacket, and the signature blond braid. This is what I learn: companies aren't interested in purchasing photos showing my (or any woman's) personal efforts on an Alaskan ridge. They want to see anonymous female triumph. I feel misleading as I keep my face low to the camera and cast my eyes onto the dark rocks that crust the ridge. I could be you, your girlfriend, your sister, your lover. Peter asks me to look at the bootpack.

At the moment that the shutter is clapping, I focus on the indented sole marks, the holes punched by other boots, the blue snow tunnels that lead each movement. Peter snaps the half profiles and the cant of my body. The staccato shutter captures my Black Diamond skis, orange against the white mountains and rocky ridge. They are slung over my back like a quiver—one dominant line. I am frozen in two-tone gray telemark boots, purple hat, blue poles, orange ice axe, bright blue shell. The rock-peppered ridge drops down and away from its spine; the valley lingers an impressive distance in the background. I have a harness pulled up over my thighs and sunglasses snug against my nose. I look confident, like I know what I am doing up in the snowy angles of the Chugach. The picture boasts competence.

Here is the truth. The snap of the shutter captured a leg that is steady, but while kicking into that snow slope, my knee shook with nerves and I fought to trust myself and the snow. The taste of anxiety soured each breath, and my head raced with questions: What happens if I fall? Am I holding up the group? Can I do this? Why am I the only goddamn woman up here? In those moments my pace stalled. With a thin voice I apologized for my slowness. Peter encouraged me, told me to carry my axe in the uphill hand while Silas set the bootpack and advised me to turn my hips to the hill. For the moment, the directions were security related, focused on the physics of weight and safety.

In the silence of that image, in the confident appearance of my stance, you can't hear my companions' strained voices or see their nervous glances responding to my fear. In fact, you can't see my partners at all. And the underlying reality is that I wouldn't be up here without them. This still frame fails to acknowledge the choreography of the setup. I slant toward the slope, set and reset each foot, jam the ice axe deeper into the snow. The axe seems to clank against rock in clumsy protest as I search for the deep, stable placement. With each move across the ridge I beg myself to trust my feet, my fitness, and my experience.

Once I emerge from the most challenging section, the place saturated with self-doubt, Peter snaps a photo. He says, "You look like you just did something." And it is true; I do feel like I accomplished something. It is the simple triumph of working through my own cloudy fear. When my breathing smooths and my body uncurls from the clench of anxiety, I say to Peter, "I hate feeling like the weak link." He says, "You have to let go of that." But I am unsure how, and he clearly can never know what it feels like to be the only woman and the slowest. In the mountains, Peter has never been the weakest link. Most of the time, I keep up, feeling strong, confident, and experienced. With each success, though, I challenge myself with harder terrain, increased consequences, and steps beyond my comfort zone. In these moments, I am most often with a group of capable men. It's not because I don't have wonderful and competent women friends. It's more a product of circumstance. There are simply more men out backcountry skiing, I have two brothers, and unless I plan a girl trip, the composition tilts heavily male. Men have become my default crew. It's not bad, it's just my reality—but I miss my ladies.

This day the ridge hosted all men. With the exception of one female snowmobiler in the parking lot at the end of the day, I didn't see another woman in the mountains. In moments like this, I feel that I have some specific role to play as the only woman, as some sort of representative of my gender. Peter's pictures document my tokenism.

With my most recent doubts on the mountain masked by his choreography, I fall into a familiar trap. I know I am strong, and Peter's pictures capture this version of reality, the image of a powerful woman. It's an uncomplicated message, without comment; my bright clothing and gear pops against a mountainous background. I want to feel that I am keeping up, that I am representing our gender in a way that is inspiring. There exists a weird pressure to mask my doubt and display that image of confidence and competence; I feel it as a tightening in my chest.

I don't want to mislead the viewers, to be dishonest in the absence of the greater scene. The photo claims my triumph, makes no comment about the company I am keeping, casts my doubtful eyes anywhere but at the lens. The product and the memory of that ridge fail to align. That is the risk of connecting image with truth.

We snake our way across the snowy route. Our team catches the group of four guided men. We move faster but stay in the back out of respect and interest; this terrain is new to us. The guide extends the generous offer for us to join them. We gratefully accept. None of us has ever been on the Berlin Wall ridge before, and the local ski knowledge is a remarkable assist. With the most technical parts of the ridge behind us, our expanded group skids down the remaining spine on our skis. We gather at the top of a steep couloir that marks the entrance to snow fields boasting thousands of feet of vertical. The clients hesitate as they look over the edge; their heads and necks lean away from their ski-locked feet. "No," one client says. Another joins the protest. Their guide explains, "It's just the way we get in. Sideslip it. I would have you on belay." Again, two of the four claim that it's too steep. The guide listens to his clients and before leaving he "highly suggests" that we enter the line through this couloir. The group moves on slowly toward an easier ski run, one with less drop and more tracks from previous skiers. Cameras remain stowed deep in backpacks as they ski away from us. The two men who refused the couloir keep their eyes fixed forward as they continue down the ridge while the other two glance back wistfully. They know we will ski it. Their group moves down the ridge to infight as we creep to the cusp of the chute.

I lean over the edge where the snow is so steep that I can't see over the roll. Sharky rocks cut to the surface—daunting, steep, and technical—but below I see the smooth and inviting terrain. I am thankful for the sharp edges of my skis as I feel them catch me. To me it looks possible: the slow slip of edges down into the gullet seems familiar. The snow is already holding me, and I know enough to not always trust the way things look. In some way, I am validating the images that Peter took, capable of being where others have refused.

This process induces thrill instead of fear, the feelings running a close parallel. Once we have decided to ski it, saying yes to the couloir settles into a giddy excitement. In my mind, I can see how the turns will look, hear the scrape of my shifting edges, and calculate the space between rock and ski, nerves and relief. I use my harness for the first time that day, and Peter feeds out rope as I move toward the throat of the couloir. The dynamics all conspire to hold and encourage me as I feather my skis between the exposed rocks, staying on my edges, belayed from above to scrape down through the steep pinch of mountain. I feel alive again, genuine. This time the outer shell mirrors the inner picture with sharp accuracy.

I untie the rope from my harness and face the remaining slope below me. Pointing my way down the fall line, my skis arc through the powder, replicating the careful s's of my younger brother. Waiting in the crisp shadows of the snowfield for Peter and Silas to join us after the runout of the couloir, we hungrily eye the cold contours of the remaining ski run. Peter has stowed his camera to ski. One by one we turn from our cluster and lay tracks in the empty slope. As the only skiers in the area, we score the run with deep, spooned signatures. We curl back into our group at the bottom of each shot to catch our breath. The snow is good and these sweet turns reward us for our hard climb. The party feels small in the vastness as we make our way down the fall line. Far beyond the edge of the view finder, the true experience is impossible to flatten.

ROOTS

Presque Isle, Maine, is not a place you visit on a whim. The blank expanses of the East do not simply funnel into this town. To end up in Presque Isle takes determination. I cross the crooked Saco River near the Maine-New Hampshire border and drive north for another six hours. I keep my atlas, flipped to the wide girth of Maine, open on my passenger seat. The long drive forces a recounting of where I am, the motion of travel inviting reflection. The question of a destination is as consistent as my search for roots. For those of us impressed with the contours of place, geography is a kind of destiny. I've just finished graduate school and I'm seeking a winter destination. I'm twenty-seven years old and again wrestling with my idea of home and place. New England feels comfortable but confining. I am afraid of becoming stuck where I grew up. New Hampshire has been the place to go back to, but the texture of the West still calls me.

Now, as I drive to Presque Isle, I wonder how familiar it will feel, how its landscape figures into my own story of place. I am going there to see Rob. We are not a couple. To everyone but me, we are friends. That definition is easier, as we tend to orbit vastly different spaces. When I am in New Hampshire, he is in Panama; when I am in Switzerland, he is in Maine; when I am willing, he is distant. But on occasion, perhaps twice a year, we make stupid, Herculean efforts to meet. He drives five hours each way for a one-night stint while I am working as a nanny. He flies to California. I drive to the West Branch of the Penobscot River in Millinocket, Maine. We do this so I can boat in roiling water and sip hot morning coffee and late night rum with him, so we can ski corn in the Sierra or share margaritas or a bed. This is the collage of our intersection. Boats and bikes and skis clutter the sheds and vehicles around us. And I just keep hoping he will ask me for things I can say yes to. I head for Maine because I have never seen Rob's home or met his family. I drive to glimpse a new piece of his life.

Aroostook County, from what Rob has told me, is a place that torments him. It represents the tradition of farming and family, a place filled with rolling potato fields and childhood memories. The fields and barns, crops and machinery store his version of home. He grew up on a potato farm, one that his family still owns and operates. This is a place to escape from but also return to. It is this sort of stifling ruralness that has seemed to trap Rob and prompt him to complain. Perhaps it is easiest to criticize what you know best. His interest in watersheds and boating sprang from the rivers of northern Maine, and the land yielded a tangible, tasteable living. When he sped down the highway, away from this home and his family, the gravity of place pulled him over on the shoulder of the road and asked, Do you really want to leave? And the U-turn said it all. Next to the guardrail of the interstate, Rob left his dream of moving south to guide the whitewater that made his heart thump. I see my own struggle reflected in the idea of Presque Isle, the familiar patterns and intimacies of a childhood landscape, the same fear of getting trapped by the shapes of home. Rob though, has placed himself in a way I have not yet discovered how to do. This is why I slam through the northern Maine darkness to him—because I need to unearth the roots of his choices.

∧ ∧ ∧

I arrive in the middle of harvest, when farmers all over the county send clouds of dust spinning from the ground. Rob has been working extra hours to help his dad. This is not his job, but in the few days I am here, Rob's time is occupied by tractors. Perhaps he is simply answering the paternal call of tradition, the push to harvest that cycled through his childhood. Even schools in Presque Isle go on break during harvest, turning the hands of the youth, raised on and around the fields, to work.

Rob, in his Carhartt jacket and ball cap, leans against a red tractor. He looks as though this tractor has molded his life. The old metal curves of the machine seem almost maternal next to him. Rob is more serious around this machinery, and his father, than I have ever seen him. Perhaps this is a product of being the only son on a fifth-generation potato farm. We stand in a huge shed with a dark, clean ceiling and cement floors. I feel small and ignorant. Tractors in storage lounge like tired animals in the far left corner, gathering the shadows of the place into their tines and levers.

In the room next to us, a welding machine whines and splashes light onto the walls. The machine shop is full of compressors and tools, dangling neatly from nails and hooks. The whole place has a look of used cleanliness. I meet Rob's dad, Jeff, in the cool expanse of the shop where he has been fixing braces for a tractor. His handshake is firm, and his hand is pleasantly hard in my grip. After I drop my hand, I immediately wish I had shaken his harder. Somehow, I want respect that I do not deserve. I am not even the girlfriend.

Rob and his father work to screw the braces back onto the tractor before Rob climbs aboard. Rob is bigger than his father and quiet in his presence. Over the mumbling engine, he asks his father to show me the farm. Already thinking of the fields ahead, Rob rolls the tractor out of the barn. Left with the quiet Jeff Smith, I follow him around in fear that I will get in the way. He deftly uses an air compressor to force the dust off his coveralls. A little smile softens his lips as he coils the hose back onto its hook and hops in his truck. I follow his lead and crawl up into the gray body of the cab. He doesn't reach for a seatbelt and I try to follow his every unspoken cue.

Turning away from the well-kept yellow farmhouse, we move slowly down the road. The truck never hits twenty as we head for the harvester. Mr. Smith does most of the talking, as this is a tour of his life work. The fields are full of his legacy. Table potatoes in numerous varieties wait in the soil to be rolled up belts and into trucks. His steady pickup pulls us into a plot that is lined with mounds of discarded earth. Rows of pale dirt stripe the big field. We approach the harvester, a huge machine seemingly run by half a dozen people.

Mr. Smith likens the harvester and the truck to a dancing pair. The two machines, although independent, have to move over the field in tandem. The potatoes pour from a long-armed conveyer belt on the harvester into the truck. The lumbering harvester uses gravity and the natural shape of the potato to help sort the rocks, dirt, and plants from the precious tubers. The brown rounds of the crop roll through a complex series of belts while people watch, pick, and throw from the rolling lines. Then the potatoes are up and into the truck, deposited in the high-sided bed as gently as possible. The only pause in the pour is for an empty truck to cut in and replace one filled with rolling potatoes.

I ask obvious questions; the whole system and scope of the farm is foreign to me. What about the potatoes the harvester misses? To my eyes it looks like there are numerous whole potatoes forgotten in the dust. Apparently, this is a small percentage of the yield, and not worth the effort to collect. This is a particularly dry harvest, Mr. Smith explains, the eighth day of harvesting in a row, and the potatoes emerge easily from the dry soil. The crew on the harvester works deftly as Mr. Smith turns his truck from the field.

Our next stop is the storage facility. I am still listening to the details of the farming life, but I have started to watch Mr. Smith. Meticulous and proud, he speaks softly because he knows I am listening, and he walks me through his work with patience. He is polite and charming, not as hardened as the caricature I had conjured for years in my mind. This is not the strict father who denies the worth of his son's choices and relentlessly asks Rob to make farming his life's work. Instead I walk beside a man who loves his farm and his son, and is probably struggling to understand choices that he never had the option to make. We enter the storage barn and my footfalls seem louder than his. The place is cool and cavernous.

"Potatoes are like people," he starts. "They're full of energy when we store them; they're living and breathing. And it's our job to store them and preserve as much energy, nutrients, and life as we can. So, when we take them out of storage to process them, they still have as close to the amount of energy they started with as possible."

The place is temperature controlled and dim. The small bodies of the harvest wait behind walls of boards—wait to be packed, wait for the machinery to once again set their lives in motion. Mr. Smith and I stop for a moment in the hallway, surrounded by potatoes. The scale of the space and the quiet box me in. He stands silently beside me in his blue coveralls, hands in his pockets. The potatoes, storage organs themselves, seem to exhale an earthy breath. Then, in one smooth motion, he clicks the overhead lights off and plunges the place into relative darkness. Before we leave, he touches each light switch again, as if to reassure himself the lights are off. The potatoes reenter their slumber.

Outside again, we watch mounded trucks unload into the vast storage lockers. Each job is specialized. A woman inspects the potatoes as they roll up the conveyer belt and into hibernation. Mr. Smith watches with an appraising eye. We continue up the road to another large field that has already been harvested. Rob weaves his tractor up and down the field, spreading thick crescents of lime. The white dust follows his long rows, reenergizing the soil for the repeated cycle of growth that will bloom in the spring. Mr. Smith parks the truck at an angle and kills the motor. He asks me what I do, and somehow writing and teaching seem like invalid answers. Perhaps I just feel the emptiness that I see reflected on his face when I tell him. Mr. Smith provides food with his living, feeds people from the soil and labor of his work. He handles the land and plants of life, while I handle thoughts and words. Mr. Smith values the touchable, edible yield, the seasonal push of the land. We skip quickly over who I am and get back to talking potatoes.

I leave the cab of his truck almost two hours after the tour started. I am stunned by his knowledge and his pride. I walk over the broken and limed field toward Rob. All the rock picking, turning, and liming is done before the winter so the fields are ready to plant when the snow melts and the spring begs for green shoots and new life. Workers tend the land, making the bed ready for the starchy flesh that stores the energy of place. Rob slows the tractor to pick me up, the machine idling as I climb on board and sit on the fender. He claims his tractor time is thinking time, and I can see that the noise and repetition could drive anyone inward.

I bounce on the big fender for two laps. I brace against the top of the tractor so I don't get slapped into it. Rob explains the trick to driving this tractor—you never look at one thing too long. Turned in his seat, his eyes flick from rpms, to where he is going, to where he has been. It is a studied pattern. The routine of checking becomes innate; as with our own paths, it seems best never to linger too long in one place lest it become habit. The scan of the panels tells him he is spreading the correct amount of lime; his speed and rpms have to be consistent. White dust shoots from behind us, replenishing the soil. He looks comfortable driving this tractor, confident and resigned. I am uncomfortable, though, so close to his intimacy with this life, these fields, and the future he has chosen in this place. This is not a person I've known before, and I can see the bond he has with the land. He is preparing it to grow and thrive, a care that was built into his childhood, into his livelihood. The sounds of the engine and the fine white dusting of lime that settles over everything are inescapable.

The next morning Rob is back on the farm with the vibrations of the tractor singing through his body. I escape to the running trails of Presque Isle. I follow loose directions and turn into the Nordic center perched on a wooded rise. Potato fields spread in shades of brown to skirt the forested area. I wish these colors felt like the colors of home, that the swaying fields could hold more possibility for me. Instead I see the dust and find my eyes scanning the horizon for mountains.

I quickly get tangled in the trails of the Nordic center and enjoy the feeling of sweat rising. I have no idea where I am headed, but I follow markers and run like I am lost, letting fear draw me forward. Somewhere, I reassure myself, I will pop out of the woods back at the parking lot if I follow the trail long enough. This has been trouble in the past, my belief that if I follow something long enough, I will find what I want. But today I continue and it works; I find the vacant lot after only an hour, and I stretch in the breeze and sunshine, happy at least for this one small success.

I meet Rob for soup before I hit the road back home. The seven-hour drive ahead already drains me, and I know my thoughts will be consumed by the fact that nothing has changed. We talk about choice before I leave. Rob says, "I dedicated some tractor time to thinking about your situation." What he means is my perpetual struggle to find where I belong, to stop my wanderings, to claim a place as my own. "I think you know where you can write, and what you need to do." This vagary hangs in the air, and I am too stubborn and proud to ask what the hell he means. I can't tell if this is a dismissal or an invitation. He gives me a hug before I head back to the mountains and rivers of my New Hampshire home.

The growl of the car through the vast expanses of northern Maine is harder to stomach going south. I had driven north to ask a question I never voiced. The pull of that question no longer occupies my time.

Instead, I think of all the confessions I didn't make while I was in Presque Isle. How much the farm surprised me, and how much Rob belonged there. And I list all the reasons I could live there, and all the reasons I couldn't. More than ever, I believe I could live anywhere, but that there has to be a reason to move. Our dreams are vessels of energy, potential stored for the future that diminishes in potency unless acted on. By the time I reach the New Hampshire border, my hope is cold. I realize that I am headed for a stint in the West to look at the mountains and people there, to look again at myself and what I want.

RECURRING CALIFORNIA DREAMS

Truckee, California—2010

This time, I have been in California for less than a month. I moved again from my native New Hampshire to explore the mountains, snow, and possibilities the West offers. I think it's my fifth cross country move—but it's hard to keep track. Standing alone in the narrow kitchen of our rental, I orchestrate a taste of New England for the holidays for my brother Jim and me. I don't feel settled here yet, so I try to make it more like home. I pick up two large onions to make Doucette meat pies, and to create something festive. It's a French-Canadian recipe from my grandmother, traditionally called *tourtieres*. I dread chopping the onions, and my fingers hesitate over the dry, thin-veined skin of the bulb. They make my eyes fight me; they turn my body against me and pinch out the safety of sight. It's just like the feeling I get in my recurring dreams, when the world dissolves into a watery slit that never comes into focus.

Solvang, California—Spring 2000

The private farm baked in the midday sun while horses in the sprawling paddocks sought corners of fleeting shade. I was eighteen and away from home for the first time, and the whole adventure was romantic. The westward trip whispered of the rhythm of movement and history. It seemed like one version of the American dream, grasped and wrestled into reality.

Earlier that day a mare had gotten colicky in one of the dusty pens. Her round belly bulged unnaturally as she lay heaving in the dirt. Her long, delicate eyelashes brushed against the grit, kicking up tiny dust clouds in front of her frantic eyes. One of the girls who helped train the horses at the farm tried to soothe the animal. With her thin wrists she moved her hands in long, slow pulls along the horse's sweaty neck. Others held an IV bag above the animal and waited, the line glinting in the sun. The mare laid her head down in the sand. The other animals in the paddock instinctively moved away; equine intuition tells a raw truth—a downed horse is a dead horse. Horses carry in their bones survival's simple equation: motion equals life.

Our group of interns had just come in after trimming boughs from the big pines that lined the driveway. Most of our labor had to do with beautification. Roses crowded the roads and the luxury of shadow in the hot California sun was cast frequently upon the paths, the fields, and the paddocks. The people were thin and tan, soft-spoken, and knowledgeable. It was a farm built on compassion, image, and the belief that you didn't need to beat a horse to train it. A horse dying in the middle of a paddock seemed awry, out of place, unexpected.

Death gripped that mare from the inside out more quickly than I knew could happen. Usually colic demands keeping the animal moving. In my past experiences someone had always caught the colic earlier and got the horse walking. But this mare was beyond the pacing and circles that normal troubles require. This horse had surrendered to the twist in her guts, following her natural inclination to roll, to inadvertently tangle her intestines more. How often are our most innate instincts so wrong?

The mare was dead before the end of the afternoon. During one of our breaks, I watched a backhoe maneuver into the pasture. I didn't realize what was happening, even with the clank of chains in the background. The logistics of moving a big animal are not gentle. And then the horse was hoisted into the air with a grunt of the machine. The animal twisted in an unnatural arch, head pointed earthward, until the chains slipped and one back leg came loose. The mare jerked and flexed, her mane swung upside down. "Don't look," one of the older girls said. But I couldn't stop watching. I wasn't sure I had ever seen anything so undignified in my life. The swinging, lifeless horse, chained and mutated by physics, hanging in the pretty California air.

Truckee, California—2010

I cut the onion first in thick slices and try to keep my head away from the cutting board. My eyes immediately start to react. I blink. My eyelids feel like they are lined in fire. I move away—away from the gasses, the smell, the wet pile of onion. I leave the kitchen to gain a safer space, try to walk it off. Putting my head down makes my eyes feel even worse—hot and pressurized. I straighten up and feel the heavy, watery pain, and struggle against my own reaction, push back the natural response of my body. No matter what type of tears spring to my eyes, my gut reaction is to tamp them down, not to let them fall. It feels like some sort of betrayal of my stoic roots to let tears in any form flow freely. Instead, no matter the circumstance, I always find myself fighting the prickly sensation to cry.

My eyes refuse to open. With my lids forced shut, I can't help but turn to my dreams, my eyes mirroring the dream state so exactly. I sink into my thoughts, into the experience of not being able to see. I have consulted what this could mean in dream dictionaries, but there is no category for it. Instead they suggest that closed or injured eyes indicate an unwillingness to see the truth or an "avoidance of intimacy." I don't give much credence to these interpretations. There must be a reason that these dreams visit me, though. My subconscious is trying to tell me something.

Castle Peak, California—2010

My focus had stagnated and I decided I needed to sweat out my restlessness in the mountains for a day. Movement always soothes me; when I can't decide what to do, I get out. Although instincts can be easily ignored, they offer little to interpret: the pull is clear. I chose to skin up Castle Peak to stretch my legs at elevation in the ever-inviting Sierra. This, I hoped, would help to settle me, give me some direction.

I worked the ridge alone. As I crested a knob, in the cool freeze after days of warm sunshine, I saw the bodies of bees. I didn't know where they'd come from. I assumed that one of the wind-crippled trees had been their home. The dark corpses, over a hundred of them, curled on the frozen snow. Their papery wings tucked up and their big eyes staring blankly forward. In a way, they were beautiful. Their bodies were intact and delicate, their poses simple and nonthreatening. I felt a great desire not to disturb them—they seemed at rest in the snow, evidence of some greater happening. I stopped in the sunshine for a moment to question the silent, dark creatures.

I am no entomologist, but the scattered forms, standing in dark relief against the icy snow, seemed like nature's mistake. Perhaps the warm weather and the length of the early December day lulled them from their sleep, making them believe it was spring. The clusters of bee bodies dotted the ridge as if caught mid-flight. It seemed sacred to ski between the striped shells. There was something unnatural about the exposed anatomy, the numbers, the bulk of their miscalculation. How could so many be wrong?

I continued on to the icy ridge, only to turn before the summit. I was alone and didn't want to press my luck. Usually it is best to have company in the mountains, someone to watch you, to provide another view. I needed to respect that despite the sunshine, the temperature had dropped. The movement in my body kept me warm as I skidded down the snowy backbone of the ridge, but I began to feel the frosty fingers of wind between my layers. It was colder than the sunshine made it look on the exposed rib of the mountain. As I passed the bee cemetery headed home, I noticed that their bodies were bent into themselves—perhaps for warmth or another type of comfort. Their darkness against the stark white called attention to the scene. Maybe the awakening and call to movement had been a mistake, a cue misread. I wondered how we could get so off track, if my own call to action could be equally misdirected.

Truckee, California—2010

I head back into the kitchen, run my fingers under cold water, and pick up the knife again. I finish the dicing as quickly as my eyes will let me. I know what I look like, with my red-rimmed eyes and weepy, stained face. When the blindness strikes in my dreams, I am driving, riding a bike, on a horse, or skiing. In my dream-world I try to force my eyes open, demand sight, regain control. I always fail. I am moving too fast.

After an hour, the kitchen starts to smell like it should—full of fat and winter and home. As I clean up my mess, scooping the onion peels into the trash, I ponder my dreams. If I can't see where I am going, maybe I should stop.

Donner Lake, California—2010

I hoist the heavy *The Secret Language of Birthdays* off the kitchen table and flip to my page, January 21st. Running my eyes down the text, I find my favorite sentences: "Perhaps their [those born on January 21st] greatest problem lies in making up their minds what it is they really want from life. Until they do so, they will, like fireflies, disappear and reappear from one spot to the next."

Fireflies, sometimes called lightning bugs, use their illumination to attract mates or prey. Inadvertently, they also draw children and lovers of magic, those who seek the snap of radiance in the sweet-smelling night fields. These bright beetles emit a cold light. They produce the luminescence with a chemical reaction, sending flickers to ride the darkness all over the world. In special situations they can synchronize their blinking. Huge communities of individual creatures ignite in unison for unknown reasons. They come together with perfect timing. They dazzle those who are fortunate to watch closely, and then they burn out. The life span of a firefly is most often two to three months. The constant show of radiance must wear on their segmented bodies. Lightning bugs, like all creatures of sporadic magic, eventually fade.

The West pulses in a similar fashion, with the promise of a new beginning, that cool beacon that is just beyond the darkness. Driving West I chase the sun and gain time. It feels right. But I never know if I will end up consumed by the cold radiance or invited in by it. Mostly, the West has been an impermanent suitor, a draw that fades, a land-scape and people who love the glitter but exhaust their bodies in the process. It's the hope that calls over the big body of the country to me, the glow and risk of change.

I am in California, the West of so many dreams. In the beginning it was land and gold. For me it was mountains and adventure. But I have reached the edge of my own personal West. In the last eleven years, I have not lived in one place year-round. The urge to move has dragged me in an elaborate and exhausting migration that is uniquely American. Perhaps I was raised to search until I find a place worth staying. Or perhaps I don't know how to stay. As I squint into the sun here, I feel a deep fear: what if the West doesn't pan out? There is a comfort to movement, and it is the instinct that I follow most readily. But how do we read where we are supposed to be?

When I change the oil in my car and prepare to motor the three thousand miles to a place far from where I started, people call me brave. Yet it is the cowardice of discontentment that pushes me into the driver's seat. This is borne from a deep-seated hope that perhaps I will stumble across what I am looking for. Following my instincts, I am feeling my way through the country, hoping to recognize a place that is innately home. It's hard to know what I am looking for, though. The whole chain of places is tiring, and I desperately want to settle, but for now I only find comfort in the looking. How wrong can an internal compass be? I want to be arrested with some inescapable quality, like the lightning bugs that find the perfect place, time, and community to synchronize their splendor and beat as one communal pulse. I want to realize the sense of belonging in my bones.

SWIMMING

From New Hampshire to Oregon, the slight jarring of the kayak worked my nerves; the boat shifted on top of my car each time I passed a semi. I glanced up constantly through the sunroof to see the orange and blue plastic shell shimmying in the wind. The straps still looked tight, but sometimes the boat shook the whole car. The cockpit caught the wind like a sail. But it never lifted off the car and cartwheeled down the sparkly pavement as I feared it might. The only reason it had made the trip westward was because my friend Rob, a boater, had said, "You'd be stupid not to bring your boat." So, with that directive, I had loaded the boat next to my two sets of skis in late August and started my journey West. I shoved my boating trepidation aside and focused on the pull of the current and the sweet rush of a good run. By the time I arrived in Oregon, I was determined to get out on the water.

I had not been paddling in years, but in Oregon, a state known for the quality of its whitewater, my kayak was my passport to a community of boaters. Lonely and new to life as a grad student in Corvallis, I ventured online to find paddling partners. Never in my life had I joined an online social site, but I was desperate to recreate an element of my old life, a connection to people who played hard in the outdoors. My apartment was stark. My kayak leaned sleepily against my balcony; skis crowded the corner of my living room. These toys and tools of the outdoors mocked my bookish start in this town situated in the valley.

I joined the Willamette Kayak and Canoe Club. I met Megi, a woman in love with moving water, at the "Cop Shop," a popular meeting place for boaters to carpool. The dingy and sunken parking lot sat between the state police and a twenty-four-hour adult shop off of Interstate 5. After a long drive on a Sunday morning, we pulled Megi's Toyota Echo into the whitewater put-in. Both of our bright kayaks were lashed to the top of her car. We would get a late start on the run called Niagara on the North Santiam River. I was apprehensive about the run, a new place, and new people. The fact that the section was called "Niagara" did not help to ease my nerves.

Water moved quickly below the banks as we pulled on stinky booties, splash jackets, helmets, PFDs, and other slightly dank gear. These pieces of clothing smelled of old neoprene and perpetually wet feet combined with the earthy tang of water life. It is the kind of smell that clings: in vehicles, in apartments, and in the wake of showers. After paddling a few times in a season the mossy smell doesn't seem as noxious as when you first start to slip into the pungent clothing. I methodically layered my body against cold water and hoped that I would stay in my boat.

An off-white Vanagon pulled in. Two men greeted Megi and started to crawl into their own neoprene and gasket wardrobe. I gave a general "hey" to the men as they jettisoned gear from the van. EJ was short and smiley, but silent. He dressed his compact frame with a rehearsed quickness. James had a calm, pale face and brown curly hair. He was skinny and stood with his hands on his hips and a slight smile parting his lips. James, without even an introduction to me, looked at my boat and said, "Yesterday two C-1ers flipped above the

Narrows and swam." I thought, *Nice to meet you, too.* James's confidence was repulsive in the face of my apprehension. Then he must have seen the spark of panic in my eyes because he added, "No one is going to die today."

I hoisted my boat onto my shoulder and made the careful carry down the rocky bank to the river. No problem, I thought, we had a good group of experienced paddlers. I was the only beginner to join the party and to stretch my abilities. The rest were squarely seated in their kayaks and their comfort zones. We sat on the dark river in our colorful plastic shells, dipping our paddles methodically in the water. Simply being in my boat made my heart thump and a tight smile was the best I could muster. My stomach churned as I watched the ease and laughter of the other, more relaxed paddlers. Despite my fear, deeply seated from a few frightening experiences years before, I noticed that the river was beautiful. Clear water pushed against exposed rocks, the clouds cracked to let sunshine through, and the smell of clean air and dry leaves swept past on the breeze. We peeled out of the eddy and headed downstream. I wanted so badly to belong to this group of smiling outdoors people. I craved the comfort and ease that I saw seep into their faces as we headed downriver. Megi was already feeling like a friend—like she was on my side. I tried to paddle my single blade with confidence; at least I could pretend to claim this river with these people. The idea of "fake it till you make it" is dubious in this sort of setting with real consequences.

The rapid called the "Narrows" is close to the beginning of the run. I planned to portage that section. James offered to paddle ahead and set up safety for the intro rapid so if anyone flipped, they would not end up washed into the Narrows. As he peeled out of the eddy, he said, "Just give me a few minutes, okay?"

Too casually, we continued to float downriver as James worked to increase his distance from us and set safety. James paddled down ahead of us, but we had already started through the class III rapid before he had even gotten out of his boat. I almost made it through that rapid, but in the last frothy hole, I flipped. In the cold, aerated water I tried to roll up, but my paddle found no purchase. The heavy river compressed around me. Underwater panic has the rare flavor of the last breath you took. After two twisting roll attempts, I decided to get out of my boat. In short, I opted to breathe. In the cold commotion, I reached for the thick black strap at the front of my spray skirt and released my body from the cockpit. This action, I knew, had bigger consequences. I had loosed my body into the bony grip of the river. Still clutching the shaft of my paddle, I kicked away from my kayak. The boat was free, and so was I.

Popping above the surface, I swam hard but made little headway. Hearing a shout, I looked up in time to glimpse James standing on the shore. Bent over his red kayak, he reached for his throw rope, but we both knew it was too late. There was no time for him to throw a rope and drag me to safety. Our eyes locked for a moment before I was sucked into the Narrows. In that fleeting instant I turned down the river to meet the swell. The specific safety directives for how to "swim" a rapid crowded my thoughts. I knew not to try to stand and I attempted to keep my feet pointed downriver. I grasped my paddle.

The Narrows is so named because the water constricts into a deep and narrow passage framed by rock walls on each side. I only glimpsed the big mouth of the rapid before a crashing wave greeted me. I felt lifted just before I went under. I sucked desperately for one last wet breath. The water swallowed me. The cold current pulled me deep under. I kicked hard in the direction of the surface, my booties heavy and my legs sluggish. The water pushed me constantly down, and when I opened my eyes, it was dark. Surrounded by the heavy river, my ears felt painful pressure while rocks rushed against and past me. The paddle I was clinging to in the beginning disappeared as the current ripped it away. I used all my limbs to combat the rapid, pulling eternally for the surface. The noisy push was dampened in my water-filled ears. Usually, by this time, I would have popped up gasping, but I found myself still in the undercurrents of the river. Alarm congealed in my brain as a singular thought: breathe. Lungs, feeling small, burned for the inhalation. My insides felt raw and desperate. I had the sense that I was traveling in the wrong direction. Then my body slowed, and I fought for air. Finally, in some sort of miracle, I broke the surface to gasp once before the current pushed me against a rock wall and pulled me under again.

This time though, I wasn't moving. The current pinned me in a rush against the rock. The water seemed calm in its pressure after the swiftness of the rapid. The river worked its cold fingers through my layers. Running through my mind in tight scrolling letters was the question: Is this where I breathe water? Is this when I drown? And just as I felt water pushing in, considered breathing despite the lack of air, the water loosened around me and the pressure faltered for just a moment. I surfaced in the swirling mess at the bottom of the rapid.

EJ was there in his little yellow kayak. He had, in fact, passed me. While I struggled under the rapid, he had boated over me, waiting for me to surface. He grabbed my life jacket and said, "I got ya, you okay?" I clung to the stern of his boat with a combination of burping and coughing. Bubbles of bile worked up from my stomach. I crawled onto the rocky bank. My entire body shook and I could not focus. My arms and legs felt leaden. I dripped and trembled. Matted strings of soaked hair hung in my face, and river water trickled from my cuffs.

James showed up quickly and emptied my boat, dumping the gallons of river water out. "You okay?" I nodded slightly as he methodically rocked the kayak across his shoulders until the boat was empty. I just sat on the slippery wet of the shore and stared at the water. Behind the slick banks of the river the trees swayed golden and ragged in the fading fall weather. Drenched, my gut was inflated with river water. My vision blurred; it gave the effect of a warped and watery world.

Megi was still walking the rapid, making slow progress carrying her boat along the riverbank. For the first time that day, EJ and James were warm toward me. Gentle concern instead of cockiness had taken over. Despite my fear, I still grasped at friends, tried to limit my weakness, to seem brave. I was content to let them think I could get back on the river to appear less shaken than I felt. My body fought against the idea of water, but I was on the opposite side of the river from the road, the river had mellowed, and it seemed I needed to prove something to myself. If I didn't get back in my boat now, when would I? So, I got back on the water. I carefully folded my legs into my boat, tightened wet thigh straps, and stretched my skirt back over the cockpit. Back on the river herself, Megi drifted over in her own boat to touch base. Savoring some deep breaths, I peeled out of the eddy and into the current. Fear flooded over me. Even the beautiful boulders and tame river could not tear my attention away from my nerves. My gestures were tentative in the face of the water and my whole body was involved in various stages of shaking. Each time the boat leaned or bobbed, I panicked. Anxiety mastered my movements. James and EJ both spent time "babysitting" me on the river; as the most experienced boaters, they were generous enough to help. They checked in, offered beta on the next rapids, and constantly reassured me. Above the rapid called Niagara, I eddied out. Megi kept paddling through the class III intro to set up safety. My stomach still twisted, I discussed the run with James and EJ. Eventually, EJ went downriver and left coaching the newbie to James.

James appeared short sitting in his red boat, his face washed with calm comfort. He looked more at ease in his boat than on land. I had to trust this man I had just met hours before, and I did. His sparkly green helmet covered his curly brown hair; the sparkles reflected what little sun pushed through the clouds. He constantly smiled and he waited patiently while I made a decision. Although I did not want to show weakness to these new people, rationale won over.

"I'm afraid I'll flip again in the intro and swim through Niagara," I told James. "What's in the intro?"

"It's a boulder garden, similar to the one above the Narrows."

I listened to the river rushing around me and felt sour dread in my gut. "No, I'm too afraid. I want to walk both rapids. Can I walk on this side?"

"No. Do you think you can ferry? I'll follow you across. Try and catch the upper eddy."

"Okay, thanks." I felt empty and relieved after exposing my fear.

Despite being a new acquaintance, James listened to my anxiety about a little rapid and helped me to make a plan to get off the river. We ferried across to river right, and I unfolded my body from the boat. In sopping socks and booties, I dragged my C-1 up the steep bank with James's help. He gave me simple instructions on where to meet them again and disappeared back to the river. My boat dented my right shoulder as I balanced it, my paddle, and the foam saddle that had been ripped out during my swim. I was soaked but warm, breathing hard, and hiking with my boat.

Each step I took, my booties squished and a bit of water seeped out. I made my way through the small bushes and trees. I used the bow of my boat to push scrub trees out of my path, moving steadily along the bank. I played the swim over in my head again and again: the dark tightness of the water, the helplessness. Why do I do this sport? I felt dejected. These new people, whom I did not know, had taken care of me. They pulled my body and boat from the water. The group gathered my kayak, paddle, and saddle. I had slowed them down and embarrassed myself. The boat weighed on my back, and I pushed it away from my body with my hip. Friends, even the wild river friends I wanted, were not worth this. I thought I was smarter.

I reached the eddy before the others and clambered down the rocks so my boat could meet water again. James arrived first. "Wow, you were fast."

"Yeah, one thing I can do is hike with a boat," I said, trying to be positive and borderline funny; I could successfully walk any rapid. I certainly preferred walking to swimming. Sliding my kayak into the swirling eddy, I climbed down and in. I watched the water drip off James's blade as I sat near the shore waiting for EJ and Megi. On the river again, I noticed that I had stopped trembling and started to relax.

We ran the rest of the section. EJ led me confidently through the last few rapids and I followed his clean lines gratefully. Megi kept me chatting and distracted with her relentless good nature and smile. I aimed for the dark tongues of water and skirted the angry holes. The bodily combat with the river had taken all my effort. Now I was slightly cold, thoroughly damp, and ready to be done. Eddying out next to the take out, I finally let my body feel the extent of my exhaustion. Even my bones felt cold and battered. We pulled our colorful shells off the dark water, strapped them onto the roof rack and shoved them into the Vanagon. Next, we put on those delicious dry clothes. Jeans and my red St. Lawrence sweatshirt felt like home—warm and clinging to my goose-bump-puckered skin. Relieved to be off the river for the day, my tight shivering ceased.

We pulled into a Mexican place around 4:30. I hammered the corn chips and salsa down and allowed food to fill that hollow place. In the warm restaurant we laughed and argued and I let the uneasiness slide away with the camaraderie.

Standing in the parking lot after our meal, I shifted my weight back and forth on legs still cool from the swim. EJ clasped me in a quick, rugged hug, and James gave a tentative embrace before piling into the van. Waving goodbye, I hoped this departure indicated the start of a friendship. I knew two more people in Corvallis.

During the drive home, with the boats whistling on top of Megi's car, I debated the chances of getting on the water again. I began to feel where I had hit rocks. In the cold rush of swimming rapids, I hadn't noticed being banged up. Tender spots emerged in the warm cradle of Megi's passenger seat. We filled the drive with talk of travel and the outdoor life. We discussed having children and relationships, her easy smile and laugh punctuating our conversation. I felt I was making a friend, this dark-haired woman who had invited me to join her on the watery veins that crisscrossed Oregon. I knew that there would be other days on the water for us.

Back at the "Cop Stop" my car waited in the neon glow of the twenty-four-hour sign. I was reluctant to leave Megi and the shared experience of the day. The end of the drive together pressed me into the darkness. I slowly loaded my boat onto my own roof rack and hugged Megi goodbye. The drive back to Corvallis flashed by as I thought about the rapid and the hazard, what I had risked to meet people. And I realized that somehow it had worked. Terrified me, but worked. These athletes, who loved the push of water and rocks, had shared themselves. I had hugged them goodbye, my hair still stringy and wet from the swim. I was shamed and beaten by the river, but this group had chosen to embrace instead of reject me. The swim exposed my fear and their compassion. They had seen me at my most vulnerable, and perhaps that was the best place to start.

Pulling into my quiet apartment complex, I took time unloading my boat. My body ached in protest as I lugged the kayak up the steps and across my living room. I leaned it carefully against the moss-covered balcony and shut my sliding door. Stepping into the hot shower, I washed away the chill of the river, the fine silt in my hair, and the smell of neoprene. I desperately tried to send my fear down the drain, too. My neck began to stiffen from the day's trauma. Looking into the steam painted mirror, I brushed what tangles I could from my hair. In the end though, with a pair of dull kitchen scissors, I cut the deepest snarls out, unable to reclaim the strands any other way.

ON THE RUN

On October 19, 2011, an Ohio man opened the cages in his private animal reserve. Then he killed himself. I heard the news yesterday and I imagine his animals—Bengal tigers, grizzly and black bears, mountain lions, all confused by their freedom. Fifty-six exotic animals loosed and not knowing what to do. I picture monkeys fleeing down asphalt sidewalks, and jaguars tentatively making their way past fences and open doors. Somewhere in Ohio claws tapped the unfamiliar ground outside the bars, while padded feet stole away without sound. But the news report said that some of the animals were still standing by their cages when the authorities showed up. That's where they were killed, idling next to their pens, bewildered at the foreign taste of freedom.

Ohio became a hunting ground for officers, armed with bullets and fear of the unknown. Not even Jack Hanna could save the animals, could halt their slaughter. Standing full-faced to the TV cameras, in the sprawl of dropped animals and cages left ajar, he offered refuge at the Columbia Zoo to any survivors. But authorities determined that the animals were too dangerous to capture or drug; the order was to shoot to kill. Last count I heard, at least three animals were still loose. Among them were a grizzly bear and a mountain lion. I wonder if the dead man had imagined that eighteen endangered Bengal tigers would be shot, that almost fifty confined hearts would be stopped. Or did he think they might actually roam free in Ohio, making the suburbs home, using their muscles to lunge and scavenge like nature intended? I wonder if he thought death was better than being caged, having just been released from jail himself. Meanwhile, schools were closed for the day, and people were urged to stay in their cars and told not to run if confronted.

^ ^ ^

I'm afraid to turn the radio on to hear if the animals are all carcasses, accounted for, slaughtered. There is a part of me that is rooting for that last trio. And I am the saddest for the animals that didn't know they could leave their cages, so they hovered near their bars in uncertainty until their deaths. Raised in captivity, their wild instincts were dampened, and in Ohio they pushed on strange ground, wondering whether to run. For me, movement is often the answer—even just to chase life for another moment.

The story out of Ohio sets my mind pacing, remembering when I worked in Switzerland and led an early morning running class with my friend, Phil. Before the sun was up, two days a week, we met at the Sportzplatz with a captive group of students. It was fall and a crust of snow had settled on the ground, the trails, and the roots we would stumble over. Frost slicked rocks and dead grasses. Sometimes the snow glowed in the moonlight, and we clicked off our headlamps in the chill morning. Those dawns before I turned a flashlight on, I found the group by their murmur, a low-throated growl of displeasure and duty. Figures stood close to each other in impatience, their hunched frames more solid than the sparse and reaching branches of the trees that lined the field. When I joined the shifting group it was exciting, like meeting for an escape, the chance to rip through the woods while everyone else slept. It was as if we were preparing for something, training our bodies for endurance and speed, fighting the classroom rituals that dominated our days.

We stomped over the same ground every time, and I never worried about anyone getting lost. But the group always got separated, strung out in the darkness. I would find myself alone in the woods. My breathing seemed inordinately loud and I felt the clarity of the cold. My heart thumped in my stomach from exertion and sometimes fear. I would create images of lurking animals to press my motivation, imagine eyes glowing and big forms moving behind the curtain of forest and morning. Passing small meadows in the woods felt like running next to a spotlight, and then I would dive back into the tree cover and work up the curl of the trail. There was a sort of blind belief moving with me—that I would eventually pop out of the woods, emerge in a safe place, if I just kept running.

The methodical placing of my feet on mountain trails seemed right, that my body was in motion, that I was already running if something were to happen. Moving in the dark pushed me with its cold, anxious edge, the seeping instinct that urged my feet faster. The woods encroached, and the brittle air punished my lungs. Isn't it always a plan in the back of our minds to just run away? I could have slept later those mornings, but instead I chose to have my legs and mind ready to flee. It's better to move than to be dropped where you stand.

∧ ∧ ∧

I didn't stay in Switzerland. I got kicked out. It was 2007 and partway through my second year as a teacher at an international boarding school. I had surrendered my personal space by becoming a dorm parent. I taught six days a week and ate every meal of every day with students. I thought that much time invested in the school would be enough to secure my place there. In the end, it wasn't. I was denied a permanent working visa. Everyone encouraged me to stay and fight. I knew, though, that it wouldn't work. I only had a BA degree and a teaching certificate. The Swiss wanted someone more special, with additional pieces of paper to prove value.

The news came suddenly. I had been told that the visa would be taken care of, that I would be taken care of. I was turned out quickly and it surprised me how fast my life felt strange and out of control. In Ohio motorists were greeted with unfamiliar messages on illuminated traffic billboards: "Caution Exotic Animals" and then the flash of "Stay In Vehicle." But in a small classroom in the heart of the campus, Phil guided me differently. "Go," he said, "go live your life." In his lilting Swiss accent his words made sense. It was as if he were cutting and prying the fence for me, hoping I would bolt. We sat on the tired classroom tables, the hint of chalk dust unsettled in the air. I looked out the big windows toward the Alps, picked out the Rosenhorn, the Mittlehorn, and the Wetterhorn. I let my eyes crawl up the mountains and remember when I climbed the Rosenhorn with Phil and our friend Simone the first week I arrived in Switzerland. Since then Phil, Simone, and I had been escaping on adventures, on skis, up mountains, and even just out the back door for a run. Running seemed to be our placeholder, an interim workout to sustain our bodies until the next adventure, the next invitation to move. Staring out the window, I climb the Rosenhorn with my eyes, taking the route we had taken. I wondered how to leave this place.

I swung my feet from the table as I listened to Phil. His woven hat carefully covered his bald spot, his sun-worn face smiled despite the fact he was telling me to leave. My hands felt dry and swollen, tempered by the chalk and paper of my life. "Don't stay for us," he said, "leave for you."

Later that week, Phil and I stood in the school's gear room. It was a narrow closet that smelled like climbing shoes. We were returning gear, clinking carabiners and quick draws onto nails, stacking ropes and shoes on shelves. Working as a team, we methodically checked in each piece, moving around ice axes, beacons, rock protection, and avalanche shovels. I was concentrating on harnesses when he said to me, "If I were younger, we would go see the world together." There was the hitch of impossibility in his voice—secured by a good job, his age, a wife, and a home. I realized that some people would envy my situation, being pushed out into the unknown. Phil was one of them.

^ ^ ^

I am just wrapping up work on the East Coast when I hear about the animals. I haven't lived in the same place year-round for over eleven years. People chained to jobs, houses, spouses, and children see this as thrilling—to be untethered and able to do "anything" and go "anywhere." Somewhere the pink gums and pointed white teeth of foreign animals are bared to the sloping green hills and cement of Ohio. Wide, yellow eyes scope out the horizon without seeing bars, fences, and wire, trying to choose a direction. Socially we are held captive by the idea of ladders, career moves, walls, shelter. I like the idea of these thick lines of security around me, but continually find myself without employment and housing, turned out into the chaos of finding my own way. I don't want to be caught idling, thinking about the warmth of my previous bed and the security of a paycheck. It's time to move again; I have the month of November to deal with. I'm expected in the west in December, with the snow. Until then I assume that anywhere else is better than where I am.

Friends of friends have a cabin in New Hampshire. They offer me the place for the month of November. I accept it because any plan is better than no plan, motion is preferable to standing still. I find the address. The cabin is on a network of tired dirt roads, placed on a slight hill amid huge, swaying white pines. Out back is a babbling brook. I tentatively move in, keeping my things in their bags in case I have to flee. I track orange pine needles and curling leaves across the carpets and into the kitchen.

I walk through each room and glance out the windows, some bedrooms so small that the door hits the bed inside, stopping the arc of hinges. The place is musty, stale from disuse. I run a hand up the banister, its railing shiny, its pine balusters hand-stripped and solid. My eyes trail over the rope-chinked logs and notice the fraying ends of rope that have worked free. The cabin feels empty. After I have walked through every room, I change into my running clothes. It's a slurry of rain and wind outside the cabin, but I abandon my sleeping computer and book to stretch my legs.

I lock the place up and cross the leaf-encrusted lawn. With the new key tucked away, I tilt my head against the rain and start up the road. My running shoes have frayed holes and my body already feels weary. But as I crest the first hill and watch leaves shimmy in the wind, I shout out to greet a pair of draft horses that are watching me from a big field surrounded by woods. They track me with pricked ears, but are comfortable, having no predators to worry about. I get my pace. I relax and affix myself in the contours of this new landscape.

Out in the open I think about the cabin and convince myself how this, too, will work. Listening to my breathing, I imagine tiger stripes between trees, eyes watching me from a perch, sleek forms crouching behind stone walls. In this unfamiliar terrain I am reminded how quickly freedom is granted and stripped. All the while I look for big cats along the road.

THRU TRAFFIC

It's 2012 and this time I am taking four days to drive the 3,107 miles from New Hampshire to Reno, Nevada. I leave Pennsylvania and my pregnant best friend, and, paying a twenty-six-dollar toll, I listen to the radio. Pennsylvania has upheld the Voter Identification Act. No documents, no voting. Meanwhile Arizona has put a damper on the Dream Act. The country is shifting before the November election, trying to find where it can settle. This is my country now, amid the big trucks and construction. In leaving Pennsylvania, I am also saying goodbye to the East Coast, and with that, finding National Public Radio stations gets increasingly difficult. I motor toward country music, toward static, toward the mixed CDs that friends have compiled, with the sound of my car engine droning away.

Until this morning, leaving Philly, home was still closer than my destination. Now I am nearing the crux, the place where turning around will be longer than continuing to Nevada. The drive, once again, has become the task of moving through the breadth of America with the intention of arriving on the other side—as quickly as possible. To witness the passage of miles without stopping to linger, to push my same self through to my terminus. The mission is just to keep moving, while sitting still, for four days.

Twined wire fence stands between the cornfields and the interstate. Every county in Indiana is a disaster zone. Drought. Forty-eight counties in all. I drive through the evidence; wilting, thirsty rows of corn line the highway. The horizon sprawls, etched in earth tones, and despite my steady progress, stretches forever away. This land is appealing in its strangeness, closer, I believe, to the moon than to my native New England. It is beautiful, yet not verdant, the sun having long ago bleached the life from its vegetation.

∧ ∧ ∧

I follow the Thru Traffic signs. In Illinois the gloaming comes in a long peach wave and does a tinted dance on my sunglasses. It even makes the tractor trailers look romantic—the glow reflecting off their long bellies. I move westward, into that promise of the setting sun, squinting at our asphalt future. The tense pressure on the gas pedal has moved up my leg and pooled in my lower back. I shift incessantly, scanning the horizon for the next version of America.

∧ ∧ ∧

Eighteen-wheelers box me into a hot rectangle of moving road. Sometimes the same trucks that hurtled past me the day before fade in my rearview. While I drive, I look at everyone I can. Today, I glanced at a young woman in a cobalt blue Chevy. We locked eyes. She was young, with hair pulled back and blue eyeshadow. Somehow, no matter how many times I cross the country, the people remain the same. They sit inert in their cars, pushing the speed limit down the interstate. Drivers look ahead, check their blind spots, and move on.

∧ ∧ ∧

I have just crossed the Mississippi River, and I welcome LeClair, Iowa, into my view. Last year at this time the river was flooding. But now, longtime residents say they see sandbars that they haven't seen in decades. I hear this report repeated on local radio stations. The high and low water marks of the year are startling—in some places a change of fifty feet. What a difference a year can make.

∧ ∧ ∧

I pass a dilapidated barn on the side of I-80. It looks like it has been cornered against the highway forever, a silent witness to the American motor stream. Cracks of light fan out through the gray slats of the siding. I notice it is still functional. Tanks and equipment to drag behind tractors wait silently for employ. Perhaps I have seen this barn before on another crossing, or will again. In my mind it becomes a fixture, another constant in the long rush of the country.

∧ ∧ ∧

One old man, just across the Wyoming line, watches me at the gas pump. Wrinkles crease his face. He has the practiced stoop of someone who has filled gas tanks all of his life. His license plate says Nebraska, and it's clear he has crossed the state line for Wyoming's cheaper fuel. I see his eyes dart to my New Hampshire license plate and back to me. "You're a long way from home," he says.

"I am."

"Are you going to school?"

"Going to teach."

"Well, good luck." His gas pump thumps off. His wife sits in the car and stares at the highway, window rolled tight against the heat, waiting for her husband. He is slow in screwing the gas cap back on before getting in and driving off.

∧ ∧ ∧

Gas is hovering around four dollars a gallon. We are in a spike after the lower gas prices of May and June. I fill my tank two or three times a day, leaving the ribbon of I-80 only to find another gas station, a convenience store, a restroom. My credit card makes my hand sweat. The Trans-Canada pipeline has started in the south. This is to carry tar sands, and according to National Public Radio, even the Texans are worried. I see the gas prices inch up while racing across the country. Some off-shore oil rigs are shut down for repair and Americans continue to fight in Afghanistan. I am driving to Nevada to take an adjunct position teaching writing at a university. The freshman students who will populate my classroom have always known the United States at war.

∧ ∧ ∧

The windmills at night become blinking red eyes on the horizon. Scores of them. I like to scan through the radio stations but often the dial spins without picking up any signal. Sometimes I find a pop station and the blaring music sounds predictably American, ever the same, but the artists and lyrics constantly renew. It's too young and fast for the scenery scrolling out my window. And then the station fades, static or country music infringes, the signal is lost. I feel like I am carrying the road now in my body, the exhausting vibration coupled with the sedentary life of the highway. My muscles, so used to the movement of running or hiking, are now stiff with inactivity. I'm nearing the end of this year's pilgrimage. The middle of our country washes past in brown and dry greens. I am watching the lingering rays of sunshine slicing through the smoke of western Wyoming. The land sculpted by agriculture is mostly behind me. The road remains the same. Soon I will pull into a rental in Reno, greet strangers as roommates, and face a new teaching job. I am slated to instruct composition and research writing classes. The future feels bulky and despite moving toward it, I am braced. For now, my eyes rest on a jagged horizon, the mountains marking west, the hazy air and rich reds and pinks crying of flame. The West is on fire—wildfires are raging in the Great Basin. Fires are stealing, and foraging, and reveling in the dry heat. Where there is tinder, it explodes.

STABILITY

Deep in the peaks of the Sierra in Inyo National Forest, I question whether the snow will hold. Stability is a constant concern. I am skinning up a groomed cat track toward what will be home for the next three days, a yurt at ten thousand feet. We ski the road into Rock Creek Lake Campground, passing signs and posts, fences and small buildings that are packed by sagging snow. Next to me is my boyfriend, Larry, and we look up into the massive valley together. We point to old crown lines, possible ski shots, and the loaded versus scoured terrain. In this tour of possibility, we are giddy with the prospects of the ski trip, but we eye the mountain ramps with caution.

Intrinsic to the thrill and fun of backcountry skiing is the continual calculation of consequences. Avalanches, the chief worry, can crack and slide tons of snow with shocking speed down a slope. The images of these potential hazards never fully leave my mind. Our intention is to spend three days skiing in this world of angles and isolation. We watch the weather for major events, read predictions, judge the temperatures. We question the winds, notice the potential loading of gullies, gauge the sunshine. We interpret avalanche reports and monitor forecasts, looking for indications of what is to come. We scout for weakness and discuss the terrain when we set eyes on the mountains. Anything for a hint of control in the backcountry.

Larry and I planned this trip almost a month ago and invited a few of his friends. As we start skiing, I am aware of the grind of frozen snow beneath my skis. No recent snow. Warm days. Cold nights. I note wind streaming through the peaks and pines. These ski conditions are not stellar. My clothing whispers with each step and I shy my eyes from the persistent sunlight. My world at the moment smells of sweat and sunscreen.

Skinning uphill, I wonder about my own stability. I think about my relationship with Larry in the language of landscape. There is so much to be interpreted: the tone of voice, a look, circumstance, an action. In truth, Larry is my first real boyfriend. At twenty-seven years old, it feels odd to be so fresh and unsure in my interactions. Before him I lived in the limbo of uncertainty and hanging out, where commitment was unsteady and nearly never spoken. Balancing the fun and risk remains mysterious, so I silently assess the stability, gauge the weather and events of our time together. Larry and I met in the shifting lift lines at Sugar Bowl ski resort. In one of the glorious weeks of daily powder dumps, I watched him scream by me with the grace of an aggressive telemark skier, the long whips of powder following him down the slope. Then he started to wait for me in the lines, forgoing the greedy laps of so many other locals. This defied the "no friends on powder days" mantra that was the gospel of powder hounds. Larry was friendly, leading me to the best snow on the mountain. I wondered if he was seeking a ski partner or more. I watched his eyes and waited for a concrete sign. He smiled a lot—but this could easily be a product of the plentiful powder, my company, or both. On the chair ride up, I tried to determine if he minded waiting for me, if he was frustrated or pleased.

Months after our first ski days together, I still watch his face for clues. After a day in the backcountry, while we speed toward home, the studs on his tires clacking against the pavement, he slides a hand across the middle console to rest on my leg. While he eyes the road, the weight of his hand on my thigh anchors me. I watch his face when I talk about leaving for the summer, wait for moments of eye contact, wonder what he is really thinking about when he chops the shallots, garlic, anchovies, for a dinner he is creating. When I try to describe what I'm writing about these days, I use the phrase the "geography of destiny," and say, "You know what I mean?" He says no, but that he would like to understand it. These moments stack in my mind as I skin towards the yurt.

With snow assessment, it seems easier. Digging a full snow pit allows me to see deep below the surface of the slope and into the concrete history of the pack. Ideally, we dig all the way to the ground. The layers are identifiable. Weather events of the past show in thick lines of snow deposited by storms. Rain and sun events arise in glassy stripes of ice or maybe the crunchy layers of crust. Then, sometimes we also find the dangerous yet beautiful feathers of buried surface or depth hoar, sparkly and angular in their existence. I poke at the snow to determine consistency. I note depths, take the snow temperature at each level, examine the structure, quality and shape, and then test. Beneath the skin of the snow waits a story.

This is the first real trip Larry and I have taken together. We are in the wilderness with two of his friends and I feel the weight of my bond to him. On some level I am on the trip because I am Larry's girlfriend; I am also his ski partner and have the time and motivation to join him. But the layers of our interactions have yet to settle into something expected or readable. Inside the yurt that smells like a pet shop, we start the trip by moving cautiously around one another. Mostly Larry and I have spent time alone. The men have an easy rapport with him anchored in experience and friendship, and their relationships far pre-date ours, which is still fresh enough that I am careful around him. On the carpeted floor, well away from the wood stove, we roll out our Therm-a-Rests and sleeping bags side by side. At night

Larry slings an arm over me and kisses me goodnight before I hear his breathing grow heavy.

On the second afternoon of the trip, after our faces have absorbed the sun of the day, we sit outside the yurt in plastic lawn chairs. The pine tree that lists above us creates little shade. For après ski entertainment we practice searching for beacons. Although we do this for amusement, it also hones important skills: it is play at serious business. Each beacon is a tiny electronic heartbeat. This safety device sends a constant signal and we wear it in the backcountry in case we make a mistake, in case we misread the snow pack and an avalanche cracks. It is a backup plan, a second chance at survival. In the backcountry a beacon sends a call out for you when you have either been careless or unlucky, when you are helpless. In matters of snow, we can exert some semblance of control, so we train.

Larry, his friends, and I take turns hiding a beacon deep in the footprint-spattered field adjacent to the yurt. All afternoon we have placed white plastic chairs with their narrow legs and sharp feet in the snow. Half the time, one or more of the flimsy legs punches through the softened snowpack and sends someone rolling. Larry sits in a carefully set chair with its feet pinching into the snow.

"Want to see if this chair will hold us both?" he asks.

In the slack afternoon, while the transceiver is being hidden somewhere in the snowy expanses behind me, I sit on Larry's lap. For a minute we freeze, wondering if the chair will hold, waiting for a leg to plunge through the sun-worn snow. It seems steady enough as I lean into him in the sunshine beneath the runways of the surrounding mountains. He smells like sunscreen and his body feels solid.

I take my weight off Larry, turn my transceiver to "search," and head out into the ragged meadow to locate the electronic pulse that waits under the snow. It's always a relief to see a group member locate a beacon quickly, move with direct steps, hold a clear path to the signal. We all hope never to need these search skills, but it's good to prepare for the worst, to practice the rescue. Accidents happen no matter how well we interpret the signs. My boots crunch over the old footprints as I watch the arrow on my digital screen shift and point. The signal is clear as I hear the beeps of my device gain urgency; I kneel in the snow to get a closer reading.

Now I am digging with the frenzy of the find. Within moments I uncover the stuff sack and mitten that cradle the beacon. I grab my shovel and return the favor by finding a new spot to sink the beacon into the snow. Larry is the next to practice the pattern of finding. I watch him from the chair as he weaves through the field on the way to his mark. We are in training to be better partners.

It's easy for me to talk about risk in terms of snow. Maybe my stoic New England roots caused me to forgo learning the dialect of relationships in the same way I have internalized the language of winter. Or is it simply that I have so much more experience with snow than I do with romance? In the snow there is a science of readable signs, tangible tests. The consequences of instability can be deadly, and there is always reason to make the conservative choice, because we can never know for sure. Propagation is important, too. If a pack fractures, will that crack travel across the slope and fan into spidery lines of instability to create a slide? Or will the trigger point crack and stay, the instability isolated, disarmed, stalled. It is the question I ask of myself as I ski toward the top of a steep gully on our third day.

At the moment, it is unclear. The gully is frozen from a cold night. The sun has beaten the ramp into a soggy shot in the previous days and now it has an icy flavor—the promise that the skiing will be poor. But at least it seems a known quantity. Moving toward the top of the ridge also outlines a simple goal: one foot in front of the other until we get there. We switch from skins to a bootpack and each step is prescribed.

I watch Larry set the steep track in front of me. With each step, he jams his foot into the snow and creates a ledge to move up onto, to continue. His skis shiver on his back as he pounds each boot into the slope. I follow the snow ladder he has built for me with appreciation:

the hardest work is going first. I admire his competence, the strength and the evidence of his outdoor passion. I glimpse it in his goggle tan and the small slice of a scar on his chin, and by the speed at which he can ascend. I like that he swivels to check on my progress. There is no way to predict the events to come, but at the moment I am fairly certain that this slope will hold and that we can manage the slip to the valley floor. The only way to truly know, however, is to release my skis to the fall line and let go.

FIELDSTONE

The sunken, cracked driveway leads up the hill to the house. It's the type of drive that takes gas; it is not a spot to coast into. Next to the turn, a Coldwell Banker sign hangs expectantly in the greasy summer air. A man on a riding lawnmower flags me down as I turn into the property. His ball cap is stained and sagging on his head, and his suspenders only magnify his bulbous gut. I roll down the window and lean toward the man, feeling a little caught. I explain that I am meeting the realtor, Jason. "I'm the owner," he says. Over the lawnmower's engine I raise my voice to say, "I'm just looking." But I feel like I have been discovered flirting, that somehow he knows I can't afford the house, that I am not serious. I don't even want people to know I'm looking. "I can open the house up for you if you want," he says. I decline and tell him I'll just wait for the realtor. "Thanks," I say, as I punch the clutch and lurch past him and up the driveway.

Jason arrives a few minutes later. I have been leaning on my car, enjoying the feeling of quiet that comes with an empty house isolated by one hundred acres and a dirt road. The lawnmower fades to white noise at the end of the driveway. Jason hands me an iced tea from Dunkin' Donuts and we move toward the house together. I feel like I could get used to looking at houses, the sweating tea in my hand, the glint of sun finding shiny surfaces. As we enter through the door with a busted hinge, I think immediately of my grandmother. The old house must smell like her home as I step inside the empty shell. On the dusty surface of a heater, Jason flops down the packet of paperwork on the place. In big print on the top of the first page is the listed price, $300,000. This numbs me a little, as I know it represents the impossible. I hold on, though, because I want to see what I am missing.

The house was built in 1948. Inside, the wallpaper defines outdated. Brown and burnt orange teardrop shapes curl into one another: paisley, I suppose, sporting lines and dots surrounding nuclei. The floors are all covered with a thick, brown, patterned carpet. It's the type of carpet that is designed to absorb and hide. The color looks like chocolate and vanilla soft serve swirled together, right before it turns one uniform color. What counts is what remains when you peel up the corner of the tired carpet. Original hardwood: potential. There is something black and sticky leaking from the heating vents in the living room. I am reacquainted with particle board. Linoleum, long dented from vacant appliances, curls in the kitchen. The place has been hard lived in.

The bones of this house seem sturdy. All the angles are sound, window sills still run a strong parallel to the floor. I think of stripping it down to the wood and windows, to see the frame of a house, to reclaim the intentional structure. It feels reckless to think about renovating a house that I can't buy, but really I want to restore it, to bring it back to the original. This house holds a small claim on New England history, authentic in a way that I crave, in a way that I see disappearing. Sometimes hot and cold water still come from separate faucets, families share bathrooms, and children chill at night because single-paned glass doesn't insulate so well. The frugality demanded by a simple home and the hard work called forth by land ownership requires the type of permanence that has always eluded me. This home would force a commitment—but then I pause to wonder if it would feel like a failure to stay. Could it be a version of settling if I chose a hilltop in New Hampshire after all my searching?

As Jason opens the basement door, I lean in for a better look through the dark that thickens and gathers below. "I can tell you're not afraid of basements," Jason says. "There are two types of people. The scared people always draw back when I open the door. It's an unconscious response," he explains. The blooming smell of mold does not greet me as I move down the steps. Instead it smells like cement and dirt, like a workspace where wrenches hang silently against the wall and cobwebs creep in the corners.

We pass through the space and I eye the water heater. The place looks as clean as a basement ever gets. Out through the basement door, a two-car garage waits. The bays are filled with pea stone and I crunch around the supports. Jason breaks the silence. "What I like about this old farmhouse is that it's not right on the road." He had often paused to let me lead through the house, filtering his responses and comments to hinge on my actions. I can tell he is good at his job, practiced at casting a kind eye, despite the fact that he works for the seller. He made this clear in the beginning, this odd client relationship where he is allied with the man on the mower. Before leaving the garage, he says there is some structural damage that he's obliged to mention. We stand facing the cement wall that makes one side of the garage, and also part of the home's foundation. A big crack works its way diagonally across the wall. Someone has plugged the crevice with a pale line of cement. I run my hand over the crack as we leave the garage to go back to the house. I like that I know about this, that I swung my hand over the seam. Somehow the crack doesn't bother me, maybe because there remains no chance of ownership, or perhaps because I expect an old house to have settled.

From an upstairs room, I stoop to look out the back window. I pull the dark green shade halfway down, and when I let go, it flips to curl back into place. How odd that the family left the curtains. I brush the curtain away and look at what really entices me. In the sunlight stand two fields—parallel and separated by a jumble of stone wall and a fringe of trees. Weeds are slowly encroaching on the grass; milkweed stands out as a different shade of green. I imagine the horses-past of this place; muscled work horses or lithe chestnut Arabians, perhaps a quarter horse with powerful haunches, head down, grazing. An old run-in shed slants into the earth at the end of one pasture. Then I imagine hay bales, the old rectangle ones, dotting the meadows in careful lines. Beyond the fields is almost one hundred acres of forest, and a wide and well-used trail draws the eye back and into the dark woods. Farther still are the White Mountains, a view perforated by the tops of trees.

To the right of the fields, in the immediate woods, stands the sugar shack. The old structure is the most healthy and square of the outbuildings. With a metal roof and defiant cupola, it boasts its value by hosting a tiny padlock. Perhaps inside, above the slab of granite the shed is perched upon, are rows of buckets and handfuls of taps, maybe a four-channel pan. I imagine the metal draped in cobwebs and creeping with rust. I imagine my childhood.

I am accustomed to the shape of cupolas. For years when I was young, my spring weekends were dominated by the ritual sugar season activities. To collect the sap from our sugarbush, my Dad used old milk storage jugs, forty-quart cans, from the dairy where he grew up. These old vessels, dented and heavy, would wait full of nature's sweet material. Dad used to pack snow around them as make-shift cold storage while he worked through the liquid harvest. As a little girl, I was involved in every step. My brothers and I rode in the back of the pickup with the cans to "collect," hauling buckets, sloshing with sap, from the woods to the truck. My feet roamed from tree to tree in oversized mud boots while my dad split the kindling and fed the half-barrel stove. On top of the cut barrel, in a four-channel pan, the sap methodically boiled away. The evaporated steam smelled of maple and wood smoke. There was plenty of spring mud, a variety of emerging bugs, life rising. I used to hang my head over the pan to feel the warmth on my face before the moisture worked its way up through the cupola. And eventually, we would have syrup at the end of the day. Sometimes late into the night, with the radio tuned to the March Madness games, my dad would draw off the golden syrup into a long metal canister where his hydrometer bobbed. The sap bubbled continuously, the roiling liquid creating the whisper of progress. Once it reached the point of syrup, he filled kitchen pots full of the hot sugar.

Forty-to-one is the ratio of sap to syrup, and this idea of evaporating the excess to claim the sweet product seemed natural to me even as a young child. The result, the buttery texture and the rich maple taste, the hint of smoke and time, speaks of the long process and careful distillation. My dad's syrup always reminds me of home, getting back to the basics of land and collection, to springtimes bursting with sugar-on-snow, soggy mittens, the battered splitting block, and the rolling steam. I'm not sure how this deep sense of the past fits into my future; I just know that it does. I feel that there is a quality of belonging to New England that demands a slowdown, a return. It's as if I am restoring myself when I look at the maple trees, think about splitting wood, or even notice the shed and cupola set on the edge of a sugar bush.

"Will your parents be helping you?" Jason breaks into my thoughts, and I drag my eyes away from the sugar house. "No, just me." And I turn again to the window and hold my breath for a few extra beats. "I always thought that I'd be looking at a house with someone," I admit. This feels like a confession, and it carries much more weight than the accumulation of the words I used. But it's a secret and slippery weight, one that is shielded behind the practicality of buying a house with someone else. Behind me Jason shifts and says, "Two incomes." I let it slide as if that is what I mean. It's 2013 and I think about where I thought I'd be at thirty-one. Looking at houses seems like a solid preview to what I thought I'd be up to, but everything else is a ghost that follows me around the footprint of the old farmhouse. By now I thought I'd be married and thinking about a family, that I would be traveling less and staying more, and that words like *nesting* would flit though my mind instead of words like *driving* and *trips* and *nice-to-meet-you*. My plans have shifted. From where I am now, I can't even see the starting-line for a life with someone else. I am weary of looking for, but simultaneously desperate to locate, that relationship.

Turning from the window, I pass a few small rooms, the austere nature of the tiny spaces pulling at my idea of home. Mostly, I look past the wooden floors and find the windows—seek views that might inspire writing. If I were at a different point, I might think nursery. Instead, I think about guest rooms and writers on retreat. We move down the narrow stairway and past the place where the homeowner could hinge a piece of plywood down over the stairs to cut off the top floor in the winter: the classic frugal farmhouse. Home is now the word that comes to mind, with the understanding of what people do to spaces where they settle.

I grew up about eight minutes from this old house, on Kimball Hill in Whitefield, New Hampshire. The directions from one house to the other include two dirt roads, one steep hill, some tar that is unpainted and cracked, and a four-way stop without any signs. This house is in the same zip code as my parents' home. Beyond my own nostalgia and an impulse, I should not be looking at this house. I even feel it as a small betrayal of Jason. It's the land that called my name, perhaps an echo from long ago of the call to my father, who grew up on a farm—he was a steward of the land.

Here is the problem. I don't have three hundred thousand dollars, and I don't live in New Hampshire. I don't live anywhere. I am a renter by definition. But the idea of tightening my belt, of investing, of working toward owning a tangible space does appeal to me. I think I would be good at living in a spot like this, mapping the trails and chopping wood, good at hunkering down, but then again, I have never tried something like this before. To own a piece of New England, the type of place I understand, to be able to say, "I own this" resonates with the person that I want to be. It fails to acknowledge the person that I am. Would New Hampshire lose its luster if I stayed? Would I still feel the urge to go West? The price takes my mind off the question of the possible, and the house resides in the very real space of impossibility. If I did have the money, the questions would gnaw at me relentlessly. I wonder if I can gain roots through this type of folly? Could everything fall into place? Could my need to move be shelved? What if this is how the doorway to my future opens? I know people who think that one idea of home can lead to another.

Jason and I go to check out the rest of the property—worth more than the house, by far. Somewhere on the plot is a pond, but Jason doesn't know where. In the honest sunshine of the morning, I pull my sunglasses down to protect my eyes from the sweep of land that greets me. We amble. There is no other way to describe our pace. Both Jason and I appreciate this walk, the history of this place, and we are pulled toward the trails and the woods, the shin-high grass pliant beneath our feet. We take pleasure in the day and the chance to be outside. To our left a rock wall made of granite fieldstone slowly returns to the earth.

We follow a worn track that leads us to a trail at the back of the fields. In the cover of trees, an old road still makes an indent through the woods. The roadbed is soft under our feet, but not soggy despite the summer of rain we've had. "These trails are perfect," I say to Jason, to myself. I am thinking about running and horses and so many other intangibles. It's a lot like playing make believe. Thinking of what could be, though, is dangerous—dabbling in the *what if* instead of the *what is*. We walk far enough to understand that so much more exists beyond what we have seen. The space muffles our conversation as we touch on land and sustenance. I say, "This place is prefect for an apocalypse. A girl would have her own forest, fields, and a spring to boot." I think, too, that beyond sustainability, this would be a good place to end up.

Jason and I return to the parked vehicles and he dispatches me with all the necessary information. Coasting down the driveway, I already know that I am leaving the house behind. The paperwork sits in a pile on my passenger seat. Driving away, I feel the steady legs of a tick pulling up my shin. I veer to the side of the road and pluck the sturdy creature from my skin. I flick it out the window and continue down the road. I let the fields of Kimball Hill fade behind me, as well as the view of the mountains, and face the treed roadways that will bear me away. Dirt turns to pavement as I put miles between me and the empty house, now far gone from my rearview. Before I get to my destination, I pull two more thirsty ticks from my body, tiny reminders of walking through a New England field in summertime. By the time I stop the car, it feels like I have lost something. Maybe it's that make-believe edition of my life, the one that has a field in New England filled with tall grass and ticks, the one that includes the indistinct shapes of a family. From that field, if I turn my back to the forest, I can see the old farmhouse, hard lived-in, blank windows reflecting the White Mountains in the distance.

MOVING

The other day Whalley sent me an image of his brain. He texted me a picture in the middle of the day after he had gone in for an MRI. Years ago, a ski accident landed him in the hospital for over a month. Although mostly resolved, the injury lingers in the shady corners of his memory. It manifests in mostly insignificant ways that only people who know him well are able to string into a pattern. Sending me a shot of his head during one of his routine checkups seems an intimate act to me, showing someone your brain. I keep pulling the image up on my phone to look again—the goofy, impossibly round spheres of his eyes, the gray and white folds of his cerebrum. I look at his name in caps in the corner. MICHAEL WHALLEY. Illuminated from behind, the tissue appears in shades of gray. I never thought I would see this man again, and now I can look at his brain. I can't parse exactly how this makes me feel. It's not like the image flashed on film can speak to my heart. Perhaps it's more associated with trust, that he showed me this beautiful, injured part of himself. Maybe if I were a doctor, or a scientist, I could glean more information from the maze of his brain. A snapshot of the inside. Instead,

I hunch toward the little phone and stare at the organ. I feel myself drawing closer.

^ ^ ^

Months before the brain text, I found myself in Bend, Oregon. This town, nestled in the Cascade Mountains in Central Oregon, was my most recent western winter destination. Including graduate school, I had spent the last seven winter seasons somewhere in the West. I swapped East for West each fall, leaving my summer job in New Hampshire for the mountains and powder of the Sierra or the Cascades. The day after I arrived in Bend, I went into the creaking cold with my friends to ski two feet of new snow. This blanket of white was so delicate that the buried rocks and roots were easy to find. My skis acquired the story of early season skiing on their bases, one deep gouge and a few glancing blows. Every passing dig and nick was worth it, worth the beginning of an entire season of ski destinations. That day, that first day, with my material life still packed in containers around my new apartment, I rifled through to find the necessities. I had yet to go shopping and had little to eat, forgot my goggles, and froze my toes. From the Todd Lake Ridge, though, I could see the volcanoes all around us, lumbering in a landscape so different from the White Mountains I had left in the East. The massive, domed bodies of the Cascades spread apart against the horizon, the cold air creating easy viewing and flushing my cheeks. The powder turns set my legs aching, and companionship kept me happy; it's a sweet version of comfort to be so content together in silence. As we worked our way up the ridges, our breathing marked our time. This tour seemed an excellent start to the move—full of potential. I couldn't help seek out this hope, a fresh horizon, a new view; maybe this time I'd stay.

It was late 2013 and within my first week in Bend, I reached out to everyone I knew or had loose affiliations with in town. Each day I spent a few hours unfolding wrinkled clothing, hanging the costumes of winter in my closet, organizing the warm layers behind orange louvre doors. I arranged a gear closet full of boots, skis, and backpacks. I let my wet telemark-boot liners dry next to the small wood stove set into a rock hearth. The studio was full of raw wood, warm colors, and a light dusting of ash. It was already beginning to feel like home.

I texted Kate, a woman I had met at my brother's wedding that past summer. Before long, I was hunting for her house on the dirt roads near Smith Rock, a bottle of wine rolling on my passenger seat floor, my headlights cutting the winter darkness. The washboard driveway jarred my rusty car and a horse nickered as I pulled up to Kate's cozy home. Early that December, she was full of nesting ambitions. Her fiancé was on a trip to Patagonia, so she was alone in their new home, also reaching for friends and community. I stepped easily into a hug; we split the bottle of wine and talked about men. A deep trust emerged as sometimes happens with a new friend. I confessed all my most dangerous desires: the hope of stopping the mad dash of my life, quieting my impulse to run, breaking the familiar pattern of movement, the sweet rush of arriving and the bitter crumbs of departure. Kate disclosed misgivings and questions too, not sure if marriage with her long-term partner was the future that she envisioned. She dreamt of passion, a fresh relationship to wrestle with, something that would ignite her soul and feel a little less expected. But she also imagined a home and being in one place.

Kate and I piled quinoa and kale into tacos. I didn't know her people and she didn't know mine, so we were free to tell each other our stories untamed by association. I was so happy to sit cross-legged on a recently unrolled rug, share simple food, lean into laughter, and mostly to see another woman my age trying to make a place. We are built the same way, athletic, willowy, and blond. We made sense as friends, too, with our humor burring in similar places. She admired the cowboy boots I kicked off in the hallway, and I noticed all of her well-loved outdoor gear cluttering the entrance. I cut the garlic into fine slivers because she had a bad wrist, and she worked fragrant herbs into olive oil. It was the beginning of an easy friendship.

Kate helped me believe that staying was possible; she had been on the move for a decade and was finally talking in the language of mortgages, paint colors, and furniture. She had hung art. She looked to the surrounding fields and wondered who had horses to roam them. Kate set up her tools in the old barn, splayed workbenches, and stowed scads of outdoor equipment. I thought that I was witnessing the happy tethering of a life. I thought that maybe I could learn something. I thought I was making a friend who was settling into the dusty town next to my new home.

Within a month, I was helping her move out.

∧ ∧ ∧

Ten years ago, Whalley and I had made an effort. We drove the arteries of New England to see one another. We kissed at the end of driveways and snuck around his mom's house in the muggy summer heat of Vermont. But soon after I was swept into the post-college grapple—for five years—working, traveling, and applying for graduate school. Whalley visited me in Oregon, where I did my graduate study. He has a picture of me on the Oregon coast that he took during that trip. I am in a blue rain jacket that is ballooned in the wind, my hair wild, as I turn back over my shoulder to look at him.

As often as possible, we used to set up a Scrabble game and listen to Dire Straits while shuffling our tiles. No commitment was ever spoken, and we drifted apart as often as we came together. Once, during his visit to Corvallis, he said I should move to Aspen when I was done with school. It was his last night in town, and we were feeling sorry about his impending departure. I let the invitation slip into the silence before sleep. It seemed too big a thought for me with a whole year of study still ahead. I let my hand linger over his heart, feeling the steady thump next to me. We were young and busy exploring what our twenties had to offer, or this is the story I created for myself. Later that year, he started dating another woman. It shut a door that I thought I had left ajar. Our emails slackened and then vanished. Years later, I found out on Facebook that he was engaged. I felt a pang of regret and remember thinking, *There goes a good one.*

In the middle of the summer of 2014, I thought of him as I drove with friends to waterski on Lake Champlain where he grew up. We passed the Old Brick Store where Whalley and I got thick deli sandwiches one summer before heading to his boat to lounge in the sunshine. Everything looked familiar driving down to the lake with my girlfriends; our plan was to speed into the evening and ski before sunset. I was deeply satisfied carving huge arcs into the glassy, mirrored coves. After the water cooled on my skin and the sun struck the horizon, I texted Whalley, "Thinking of you while waterskiing on Champlain. And congratulations, I hear you are getting married." He didn't text me back.

^ ^ ^

In January 2014, after a day of helping Kate escape her former life, an afternoon of packing and shuttling books and art in the languishing Oregon sunshine, Whalley called. We talked for an hour. He never mentioned his engagement, and I thought it odd but didn't bring it up: the possibility that he was not getting married was too edged with delight. I had thought he was calling to get my address for an invitation to his nuptials. After we talked, I had two glasses of red wine and wrote him an email. I congratulated him on his engagement, saying that it was hard to find someone for the long haul. He responded while sitting at a closed airport café, waiting for a flight. He said that it was tough to find someone for the long haul, and to that end he would not be getting married this year. He wrote, "Maybe it was a mistake that we didn't chase what we had years ago." His email stirred me, and I proposed a ski trip so that I could veil this second chance in something familiar. I was afraid to load the visit with expectations, so instead, I couched it carefully in potential powder turns. If nothing else, I told myself, I would get some good skiing. I watched the weather forecast and wondered how it would be to see Whalley again. The winter spooled out in front of me. In Aspen, the weather report called for snow.

∧ ∧ ∧

Sometimes what appears solid on the surface is, in fact, malleable. It was Kate's choice to end her engagement. Her ex wanted the house, so we hustled to remove her from the space before he returned to the States. When I arrived that first afternoon, Kate looked tired and overwhelmed, her hair pulled back tight with a halo of strands that had worked loose. Wrinkles stacked below her eyes, and the house lay in full disarray. This first of the moving days we tackled her closet; Kate ran her hands over her clothing and began. We worked our way through the dresses, shirts, pants, and jackets. I sat on the floor and folded. My jobs were folding and talking, to keep the rest of the voices at bay. Piles grew around me: Goodwill, costume bag, winter, Africa, Hawaii, long-term storage. Also, a stack near the door of cast-offs I should try on. The day was punctuated by Kate's heavy sighs and impossible questions after splitting from a man she had been with for almost a decade, their lives and careers beyond ensnared. "What do I do with this?" was the most frequent question.

With the desert spires of Smith Rock sitting not far in the distant dark and the hum of the washer pumping in the next room, I tried on her cast-offs. Our coloring is the same; the grays and blues pulled at my eyes. She is shorter than I am, so she ended up folding the pants back into her life. I took a few sweaters, a technical fleece, and a pair of girly shoes I may never wear. I slipped Kate's life on, the smell of her inseparable from the clothing. Loud country music cranked from a mostly packed room down the hall, the Dixie Chicks stoking our energy. Most often we worked at the same task, choosing the company and closeness over the growing emptiness of the house. I slouched at the sink, washing the fine silt of camping from her mobile kitchen. She dried and repacked the Tupperware box, pausing to make a knife guard. She protected the serrated blade with duct tape and cardboard, preparing it for a safe slumber. In our conversations, I supported her choice to leave, helped to pack her bags so she could flee. I didn't know her ex so I easily placed my faith in her choice—I felt it was better to cut and run before the vows. I never saw her cry. It was a dry-eyed perseverance that masked her face, but I felt the weight of the situation, far beyond the boxes of books we moved and the cumbersome bones of her domestic life. Packing to move is always this way, the sloughing of one life and the gathering for the next. What is kept and what is passed on hinges on intangibles like memory and hope.

Kate wondered who her friends were, the split was so divisive. Who would show up for her? The following days we moved most of the furniture out of her house—the butter-colored chairs and the worn leather sleeper sofa. The comforts of the home disappeared as we rolled up rugs and stuffed pillows into trunks. She waffled over the metal killer-whale wall hanging that they had bought together. Its edges were sharp and full of movement. Eventually it found a home tucked between some tablecloths. What of the gifts? Him to her? Her to him? Wooden bowls nested in the dish drainer waiting to be packed or left. We wrestled shapes into her truck and my car. We took laps to the storage unit. In the afternoons, we drank wine.

Duress settled into our days of packing and moving, the feeling that we just had to get through it. Mixed in, though, was that sliver of hope. It was the bullet dodged. Somehow it seemed like Kate had escaped something just in time, and I watched the spark of her fresh romance flare and catch. It was amplified by the chance to start anew. And sometimes amidst the work, a giddiness emerged. Laughter gurgled up unexpectedly while we shoved a futon mattress awkwardly into her truck bed. We smiled at a beautiful print that her fiancé had given her and tucked it into a stack of things for him to find upon his return. She hung a postcard over the spot where the metal killer whale had been, a small placeholder for the absence of so many things.

I realized that I was a natural choice to help Kate move. I was willing, and my schedule allowed me to show up for hours at a time. That, and I was good at it. The first day, the day of the clothing, I brought espresso cupcakes and fancy coffee to help get us through.

I was quick with a sharpie to label boxes. I moved my own life every six months, and through repetition, I had become accustomed to the culling process of transitions, identifying what should be kept and what to let go.

It just so happened that I also claimed no long-term romantic relationship. Almost perpetually single, I was a runner. I understood motion in my bones. Maybe I could better understand a broken thing because I did not have an intact one. I would show up to help out, to do the tangible work of moving. This was something that I could give. It sunk us into a friendship where the weight of belonging and conversation melded us together. It was also the best I had to offer, the manual labor of moving. I supported her blindly as I stuffed shoes and boots into a backpack, carted bags and totes to my Subaru. Later that night we escaped from the dust and heavy boxes to eat sushi: bright pink flesh, fatty stripes, white rice, and thin ginger to make us feel clean again.

∧ ∧ ∧

At the end of January, just after pulling down the metal storage unit door with Kate and hugging her goodbye, I boarded a small plane that whisked me to Denver. I claimed my battered ski bag and met Whalley on the curb. I wore a soft, gray wool sweater, one of Kate's cast-offs. When I saw him step out of his truck, my hands were full, and all I could do was lean into his embrace. It felt both odd and familiar. We holed up in his uncle's vacation house in Aspen during a snowstorm and set up the Scrabble board. I chopped veggies on the butcher block and we crafted simple dinners. It seemed like an escape. The first night we both had trouble sleeping. Maybe it was the altitude or maybe it was sharing a bed again. In the early hours I scooted right to the edge of my side of the huge king mattress, begging for sleep and for my busy thoughts to settle. At four in the morning I slipped into the big bathroom to take a shower and hope for a reset, the fan humming above me as I let the warm water relax my sleep-deprived frame.

The next morning, we skied one of the biggest single storm cycles in Aspen since the eighties, gasping for breath between deep powder turns. On the lift up, he knew when I was chilled and pulled me closer to him. We hoofed it up the Highlands Bowl to lose skis and smile like crazy in the tree shots. After a day spent on the hill, we crowded into the tavern at the base lodge to jam greasy pizza into our cold bellies. He introduced me to his friends, recklessly. I noted the surprise on their faces, the questions piling up behind politeness. I was sure that the easy affection between us was evident and his friends craved the details.

The evenings brought a quiet that I associate with snow, the steady, silent fall of endless flakes. Some nights we sat steaming in the hot tub, watching the white blanket settle onto the landscape. Often, he sought out my hand, and we were linked in the quiet of the storm. I left Colorado wondering if it was the snow or the company or both that had me elated. I found myself telling my girlfriends that he took care of me in a way I didn't even know I wanted.

∧ ∧ ∧

I met up with Whalley a few months later in Florida. I left Bend with the flush of spring on its cheeks. I hardly told anyone where I was headed—my relationship was too new and fragile following the wreckage of moving Kate. On some level, time with him felt like a refuge, something to be protected. We joined my friend, Jessie, and her extended family. We shoehorned into the beach house with eight kids and five other adults. I witnessed Whalley's joyful interaction with the children, like a child himself. We lounged in the ocean, letting the salt water and sun blaze our skin, catching waves to be run aground by the surf. In the afternoons, we played Scrabble with my friends and drank cocktails, waiting for the time to cook grouper and smile into the night. I laughed so hard that tears rolled down my cheeks. While we watched the sun pierce the ocean, he put one warm hand on my shoulder and dug a careful thumb into my tired muscles. Repeatedly, I leaned into him. On the boat ride in the choppy ocean, he kept a hand on my waist as we bumped through the sunshine. Later we split a beer and I felt young.

The night before he left, he said, "I'm in love with you." The light was still on, the frogs outside gleeful with noise, the house quiet.

The gray corners of his brain may not allow him to remember, but it was the second time he had said it to me. Years ago, it was through a long-distance cell phone call. After a summer spent together, before he departed for New Zealand or maybe after he was already there, I can't recall, he said "I love you." That time I said, "Thank you." He said, "I just wanted you to know, that's how I feel."

With the waves rolling up on the sand and the night critters singing, it was too fast for me. I could feel the panic rise, the push to run away. I squelched it. "You are brave and wonderful, but you need to give me more time." What I should have said, maybe, was, "Let me savor the falling."

We woke at five the next morning so he could catch his Uber to the airport. I kissed him goodbye, my mouth still tasting of garlic from dinner the night before. He turned the light off and I moved into the warm part of the bed he had just vacated. I listened to the heels of his cowboy boots tapping the morning quiet and then out the door and onto the crushed shell driveway. I heard his steps crunching until the car door slammed. The last impression of him was the moving slice of headlights that roamed the walls as his car turned and left the driveway, bearing him towards Tampa. His plane would speed him West; our next meeting was indefinite. I spent the whole next day missing him, my mind busy. I acknowledged my capacity to flee and wreck something lovely. I tamped my impulse to bolt. Two days later I flew back to Bend, arriving to snow and my sweet studio apartment, back to Kate, back to a cold stove and a quiet longing.

^ ^ ^

After six months in Bend, the time of year descended when I only kindled a fire occasionally. I started to refold my clothing, to pack again. I punctuated the sorting and cleaning with long runs on the riverbank of the Deschutes. Trees exploded in flowers all around me, spiky grass thriving, spring ripping into the forecast. It felt wretched to be leaving again. For the last seven springs, though, I had packed my car on the West Coast to drive East. At the very least, I was enacting a familiar and comfortable pattern.

Kate had already moved on to live in her shiny Airstream somewhere in the mountains. I could picture her home-on-wheels parked beneath a classic climbing vista, the sun slamming into the silver metal, dust working into her life, and a dull comfort in being transient again. That same uprooting companionship, the familiarity of movement and highways, would soon be mine again.

One of the last nights I was in town, I had dinner with a friend at her new place. We threw together a salad with refrigerator remnants and drank ginger beer with bourbon, a wedge of lime floating in the amber fizz. We ate good bread with generous butter and chatted into the evening. On my walk home, a ten-minute jaunt through the quiet streets, I called Whalley. He told me he wanted to buy a house in Denver and asked my opinion. "I know this is loaded," he said. At the time, we had been seeing each other for four months and I felt the rush of the timeline. Tasting the sweet ginger beer in my mouth, I hesitated. I felt like this decision belonged to him. I was wary of the brick and mortar commitment, of buying a city house, of encouraging him in one direction or the other. I felt too far away to whisper, "Don't do it," but that was my own fear of weight, not his. I walked straight through a sprinkler trying to find what I wanted to say. He filled the silence instead: "The only thing that concerns me about this choice is how you might feel about it." Finally, I told him that he needed to make the right decision for him, and that his reasons were sound. This felt like a cop-out, like I wasn't investing in our future, but the gap between the dark streets of Bend and a new address in Denver yawned too wide. I wanted to be the type of girlfriend to rejoice in the chance of a home, but I was still learning how.

I finished that week by loading my things into my Subaru again, the door of the house propped open to the sun, to the full summer that had invaded Oregon. The first stop on my cross-country drive this year was to park my loaded car in Whalley's driveway in Denver. He was still in the dank rental and wanted to escape.

∧ ∧ ∧

Whalley bought himself a house. One afternoon he held the phone in front of him as he gave me a FaceTime tour. The hardwood floors drew my eye along their golden planks, only a little uneven from one room to the next. The camera swayed with his steps, the Colorado sunshine pushing in through the windows. The family who moved out left the floor-length brown drapes, mirrors in the bathrooms. Little else filled the shell of this new space—it seemed to be waiting.

Downstairs, he walked the camera past the exposed brick walls of the kitchen and out into the backyard. The gardens, in neat raised beds, had plants plumping in the sun. Yellow squash, green tomatoes, peppers, and onions all waited for ripening. The cantaloupe had started to sprawl. I contemplated their roots, fastened to the soil, allowing a simultaneous holding and stretching of their plant bodies.

Over the Fourth of July weekend, Whalley flew East to see me. We participated in the expected family circus of meetings, driving the rural roads between Vermont and New Hampshire and grilling with family and friends. He drove my car around the streets that bound his childhood, while I sat content in the passenger seat watching horses graze in the lazy sunshine, the carefully tended fields rolling out the windows. On one of these drives from Burlington to Shelburne, he reached for my hand and said, "I wanted to talk to you again about moving in with me." I held his hand loosely in the summer heat. "I've been thinking about it," I said. He filled the silence again, "I know I'm asking a lot. But we don't have to be there forever." Instead of imagining a place for my next winter destination, I imagined a person. That Whalley could be my next stop, my winter location. Maybe, even a place to call home.

We drove up to his Mom's big, quiet house in Shelburne, where he grew up, to look at pieces of furniture for the new house. I found myself standing back as Whalley ran a hand over an old coffee table, tilted open an antique ice chest, assessed a collection of tiny model cars, and eyed a trunk that lived in the garage. I tried to weigh in when he questioned me, but I'd never before been invited to move, never before thought of building a life around furniture that was not rented or temporary. It whispered an uneasy permanence. I helped him pile the things he wanted to go West. I hardly felt a part of any of it. It wasn't until after he went back to Colorado, after he was two thousand miles away, that my decision came into focus.

∧ ∧ ∧

Back in Denver, Whalley made the dining room table himself. The solid oak piece came to fruition in the new garage on weekends and evenings. Whalley stood in sawdust and listened to the whir of his tools. I pictured him there, standing on the cement floor among his saws, planers, and sanders, happily building the smooth surface that so much of our life would rest upon. When he answered the FaceTime call, he smiled, flicked off the saw, and tilted his safety glasses up. He told me about his progress, promised to make me a desk where I could write.

Late in October in the fraying days of fall, I began to pack again. I drove a carload of my things to Whalley's childhood home in Vermont. With the help of his mother, I loaded pieces of my life into the square metal container that she would ship to South Grant Street. Alongside other pieces of furniture he wanted, I jammed my tent, sleeping bag, and sleeping pad into a deep set of shelves. Puzzling together my flannel bedding and boxes of my ski gear, we slowly closed the space around the bigger items—padding with rugs and pillows. Blankets eased the edges of side tables, the antique ice chest, and the trunk. Back in New Hampshire, I pulled clothing from hangers that swung in my empty closet. I bought extra Tupperware boxes. I folded endlessly, made a pile for the consignment shop, and for the first time in years I nestled art between the soft stuff of my life. I had room for the extras now. My tennis racquet rode pressed up against the window, my kaleidoscope of summer clothing sat in bright layers in the back seat. My three sets of skis, which I didn't trust to the shipping container, topped everything off, the tele bindings tapping as I drove. This was the first time ever I had shipped my belongings West; my car could no longer contain my move. Still, the westward migration settled in a familiar way around me. I drove my laden car slowly through town, my houseplants starting their long shimmy on the floor of my passenger seat. As the miles between Colorado and New Hampshire began to roll away, I tried to quiet the familiar angst with my rising hope.